WRITING FROM SCRATCH

WRITING FROM SCRATCH
For Business

ARTHUR G. ELSER

JOHN CLARK PRATT
General Editor, *Writing From Scratch* Series

Rowman & Littlefield Publishers, Inc.

ROWMAN & LITTLEFIELD PUBLISHERS, INC.

Published in the United States of America
by Rowman & Littlefield Publishers, Inc.
8705 Bollman Place, Savage, Maryland 20763

British Cataloging in Publication Information Available

Library of Congress Cataloging in Publication Data

Elser, Arthur G.
Writing from scratch : for business / Arthur G. Elser.
p.   cm.
Bibliography: p.
1. Business writing.   I. Title.
HF5718.3.E48   1989
808'.066651—dc20   89–12516 CIP

ISBN 0–8476–7632–3

5   4   3   2   1

Printed in the United States of America

Contents

Preface

Why read this book?

So you think a book on "Business Writing" can't be fun? Think again. As the testaments from two of America's leading corporations show, *Writing from Scratch: for Business* delights as it instructs, and whether you are already in the work force or aspiring to join it, this book is just what you need. And as you'll find out, it's good at least until the year 2213.

As the author shows by statement and example, precise communication in business is not only required for advancement but is also the actual source of power and responsibility in the corporate world. Lost contracts, botched orders, disgruntled employees, shattered dreams—all of these kinds of failures have often resulted from communications gone awry.

What this book can do for you.

By showing you how to conceive, draft, write, revise, and transmit business proposals and instructions, both in-house and to the outside, this book will give you the basic tools for any kind of correspondence you'll have to create—and if you remember Elser's "Killer Rules," you'll always be able to get your point across to the people who really matter.

Unlike other "How-to" books, however, *Writing from Scratch: for Business* also gives you an insight into how corporations operate, and while you, the *real* author of the memos and reports that Elser helps you write, struggle and succeed with your assigned communications, you'll learn an important lesson about survival in today's—and especially tomorrow's—business world.

John Clark Pratt
General Editor

Chapter 1

The Killer Rules of Business Writing

Two YEARS AGO, I spoke to Tracy Newnam, the engineering manager of Lovejoy Electronics, a firm which had run a classified ad for a technical writer. Lovejoy designs and builds electrical and electronic equipment that accurately controls the speed of electric motors. Although I had been writing technical books for many years, I had no experience with AC motor speed controllers and was a bit nervous at the start of the interview. I had looked at Lovejoy's earlier manuals and discussed with Tracy how and why the manuals I would write would differ. The earlier manuals seemed to have been written for engineers rather than for the electricians who would install the equipment and adjust its operation.

When Tracy questioned my suggestions for change, I mentioned that installing these controllers did not require understanding the electronics of the equipment but did involve a step-by-step process that needed to be done correctly if the equipment was to work properly. He agreed, and I asked if the manuals I had seen were typical of industry norms. When he said that they were, I mentioned that Lovejoy's marketing and sales staffs could use a well written and adequately illustrated manual as a sales tool. A customer's factory manager or foreman could look at the installation and operation manual and see immediately how simple installing and adjusting this controller would be.

We then discussed the technical support Lovejoy provided for its customers. When Tracy mentioned that the one engineer who handled technical support was usually swamped with phone calls, I mentioned that my manual could be so simple to use that the number of technical support phone calls would decline. He said he was delighted—because he had planned to add another support person just to handle customers problems in installation and operation of this new device.

When the interview was over and I got up to leave, Tracy asked what I thought about the earlier manuals. I said I thought they were hard to find information in and added that the illustrations were too complex and weren't referenced well in the text. He laughed and said, "I wrote them." I knew I had just blown my chances of getting that contract. A few days later, however, I got a call from Tracy's secretary who told me the contract was mine.

Several weeks later at a meeting of some technical writers, I spoke to another freelance technical writer who said she had bid on the Lovejoy contract and was surprised to learn I had gotten it. I was surprised too. She had a better technical background than I had, although her writing experience was similar to mine. As I talked to her, I realized she had not recognized the problems with the earlier books. She would have produced manuals that looked exactly like the earlier ones. My edge was that I had pitched my proposal around my "killer rules." Although the books to be written were technical ones, I had won the contract because I had a better understanding of the business aspects of how the books provide help for marketing, sales, technical support, and the customers. I followed some rules she hadn't. The distinction between technical and business writing is mainly in the subject matter. Technical writing deals with the facts of engineering and scientific operations. Business writing deals with the facts of customer service, finance, marketing, and personnel. The techniques are similar in both types of writing—only the content differs.

How well you succeed in business writing will depend on how well you apply three simple rules. I call them "killer rules" because you will get killed in business if you don't heed them. What are they? Well, *before you start to write,* make sure that you clearly

1. Understand your *purpose.* You may have several purposes, each needing a different memo or letter.

2. Identify your *audience*. You may have several audiences and need to write different memos or letters to each of them.

3. Identify your audiences' *needs*, and meet those needs as you write. This may require special treatment for each memo and letter you write on the same subject.

Although both of us who had written proposals to Lovejoy realized that our purpose was to get the contract, I also realized that the audience for my *proposal* was not the audience for the books I was to write. When I wrote my proposal, I addressed not only Tracy Newnam, the engineering manager, but also the sales, marketing, and technical support managers. I knew that they too would read the proposal and were also interested in manuals that would support their needs. I had learned from Tracy that the president of the company would make the final decision. He would be more interested in how the proposal would affect the company's bottom line than whether or not I could write better than my competitors. Because I applied the killer rules, I got the contract.

In this chapter we'll explore how these rules apply to the everyday world of business writing. You've seen how I used the killer rules to write a proposal. Now, let's see how I used these rules as I started thinking about writing this book.

My purpose in writing this book.

As I sat down to write a proposal to Rowman & Littlefield, I had to make sure I understood my purpose in this book. After all, if I didn't know what *WFS: For Business* is about, who would? The purpose, I decided, was to write a book that would

- Tell you about the Killer Rules of business writing

- Give you a disciplined process to follow in business writing

- Let you learn how to combine the killer rules with a disciplined writing process by following me through some practical written exercises

- Show you how the rules and process fit into everyday business situations.

In other words, my purpose is to write a usable book that contains the tools you'll need to learn to produce effective business communication.

Who is my Audience?

Once I had determined my purpose, I had to determine who you are. My editor and publisher helped me with that. They told me you are either a college student who is taking a business writing course or a business person who picked up this book as a tool to help sharpen your writing skills. There is also the possibility that you are a business-writing teacher who is looking for a text your college students will find useful and usable.

If you are a college student reading this book, I've assumed you are between the ages of 20 and 22 and a business major who hates to write. You've had a basic freshman comp course. Writing makes you nervous. You are a reasonably intelligent person who intends to strive for excellence and success in the business world. Articles you've been exposed to in your business classes have stressed the importance of being able to communicate clearly, and because of that, you are either taking a class in business writing or have picked up this book hoping it will help you hone those skills.

If you are a person already in the business world, you've bought this book because you already know the importance of clear writing. Perhaps you feel a bit uncomfortable with your writing skills, and you may have suffered some setbacks or embarrassments because of weak writing skills. You may have tried unsuccessfully to improve your writing and have become discouraged with the books and classes you have tried. You have not yet found the right methods.

If you are a business writing teacher, you might be looking for a classroom tool to help you translate ideas about clear writing found in the typical grammar-and-logic-oriented text into a practical set of rules that work in the business environment. You know that students promptly forget grammar and logic rules the moment the final exam is over, and the student who wrote excellent papers for you one year is turning out bureaucratic drivel the next. You'd like to have a more positive influence on the professional lives of your students. I've been in your position, and this book is the result of my search to reduce the hopelessness I've felt when trying to teach business writing from the traditional text. We must teach process, not grammar rules or forms, if we are going to help our students write better.

What do you need from this book?

Many of you want to be motivated to learn to write better. We've all had composition courses that left us feeling that writing was an art only a few would ever learn. Often our comp teachers fostered that idea with snide comments about our writing abilities made in red pencil in the margins of our papers. So, I must somehow motivate you to try to learn to write well and must keep you motivated throughout this book, and keep you motivated to write well for the rest of your business life.

Finally, you want a process you can follow that will guarantee success in your business writing, not a set of three hundred grammar rules used to point out errors in your work. You need a process that will keep you from making those errors and help your written correspondence communicate. You want your boss to notice that you always get your point across and get the job done quickly and efficiently. That's where the money and personal rewards are.

You are either about to embark on a journey into the business world, or are already afloat (I was tempted to say adrift) in the business world and need some idea of what's ahead and how to handle it. So, let's get on with the first part of the writing process, putting the killer rules of business writing to work for you.

Decide on your Purpose

Unlike your experience in many composition classroom situations, when faced with writing in the business world you will usually have a pretty good idea of why you're writing and what you're writing about. For example, your boss has given you a project to manage or implement, or a customer has complained about a product or service, and you must placate someone. Each different writing task has a real context that you must deal with. You're not writing about the symbolism in a play, the motives for one country attacking another, or the psychological phenomenon that causes kleptomania. You're writing a proposal, for example, that might determine the financial success of your company for the next two years.

Typically, your business writing will have four general purposes. You will provide *information* or *give direction* to others. You will *react to direction from others*, or you will try to *persuade and motivate* others. Usually, you will not be able so clearly to categorize your correspondence, but one of these categories will provide the primary focus for your writing.

Providing Information—For example, you may have to write a report to provide technical or financial *information* about a product line or other aspect of the business. The Vice President for Marketing may get this report quarterly, and it is your job to write it. At other times you may be asked to provide periodic progress reports about a special project on which you are working. If you run into problems with the project, you may have to provide details about the problem to the senior staff. When customers write to learn about a product or service, you will have to provide that information.

Providing Direction to Others—Whether you are in a managerial position or working for someone in such a position, you often will have to write to *provide direction to others*. You might write a set of steps for someone to follow to accomplish a process, such as a method for establishing a line of credit for a customer, or a procedure to be implemented for establishing a new vacation policy. Or perhaps you'll direct people to stop using a procedure and start using a new one that saves the company money. At times you may assign tasks to others and want to be clear about those tasks and the procedures used to accomplish them.

Reacting to Others—Unfortunately, there are those times when you must *react to others* because something has not gone according to plan. You must answer the memo from an angry senior manager asking why the budget didn't include the new computer software he'd asked for this year. Or you must explain to an irate customer how the company will make good on a defective product given as a wedding present. When rumors circulate about layoffs, you have to get information out to counteract the fears caused by those rumors. On the pleasant side, you may want to write to a subordinate telling how pleased you are with the way he or she handled a certain difficult task.

Persuading and Motivating Others—Resistance to change is one of the most common problems managers face in the business world. Workers, comfortable with their jobs, see new policies as somehow threatening. You will have to write memos explaining new policies and their benefits to employees. You will have to *persuade* others willingly to do your bidding so that new policies take effect smoothly. Perhaps times have been rough and you want to *motivate* your subordinates to hang in there a bit longer and give a little extra to get over the hump. Writing to explain new policies or to ask more for more effort from those already tired is difficult, but necessary. Often, problems in business arise because no one took the time to write.

As you can see from this discussion, your writing may easily have multiple purposes. You must, however, not let myriad purposes keep you from identifying each one of them and clearly defining it *before* you start writing. You must be sure to address each purpose in the appropriate memo, letter, or report and not muddle your correspondence by inappropriately mixing purposes. For example, you may decide that you must write a memo that directs and motivates a staff group to start using a new computer based procurement procedure. The next two rules will help you decide which purposes to achieve in which pieces of correspondence.

Consider who your Audience is

Once you've decided on your purpose, you must consider the person or persons who will read the correspondence. Realize that to communicate to your reader, you must use language and terms the reader knows. How readers respond to what they read depends on age, education, position, experience, and attitudes. The article in *Scientific American* that tells how the Romans used numerology in architectural designs is fascinating reading to the archeology major, but the computer scientist might find it dull.

An article in the *Harvard Business Review* that deals with a management style you are particularly interested in would bore your friend who is an electrical engineering major. If the *HBR* article, however, appeared in *IEEE Spectrum,* was placed in a context of project management, and discussed how a small computer firm used the management style to achieve breakthrough performance on a new computer design, your friend would probably photocopy it after reading it twice. Our response to something we read depends largely on our interests and whether it is written on a level we can understand. As a business writer, you'll need to consider your audience as you sit down to compose each piece of correspondence.

What characteristics of your audience must you consider? Which are most important? Which characteristics will determine your choice of terms, language, and examples? These thoughts should go through your head every time you sit down to write. Telling your parents in a letter about the latest project you are working on requires different ideas, language, and terms than does writing a progress report on that same project for your manager's boss, especially if your parents are both elementary school teachers and your manager's boss has a PhD in the discipline in which you're working.

Position relative to you in the organization—One of your first considerations about your audience is its relative position to you in the organization. I'm talking here about *tone*. Obviously your tone should never be condescending or obsequious, but it can have more or less authority in it. When you ask a senior vice president for financial matters for permission to change an accounting procedure, your tone will have less authority than when you are directing a staff to implement that accounting procedure. Explaining the new procedure in a memo to your peers in other functional positions will have a more casual and friendly tone. Some of your company's people you'll write to might be

- Hourly workers who do repetitive, unskilled jobs
- Hourly workers who are highly trained and skilled
- Salaried workers who are administrative staff members
- Salaried workers who are technical staff members
- Managers and executives
- Customers who buy your products or services
- Vendors who sell services or products to your company

These readers have different characteristics which will affect how you shape your message to them. If you fail to consider these factors, your message will be garbled at best.

Educational background of your audience—You must consider educational background because you may have to explain terms and concepts to some readers and not to others. For example, if you are explaining how Return On Investment was a major factor in a decision and you are writing to a group of brilliant PhD scientists, you may have to explain ROI and how it is calculated. Writing the same message to a group of business managers wouldn't require an explanation at all, only the numbers used in the decision. Although technicians deal with similar pieces of equipment and designs as engineers, they don't have the engineer's theoretical background. You must account for these differences in educational levels as you write. Consider the educational background differences in this list of possible readers:

- High school graduates who have little or no additional training
- High school graduates who have extensive technical training
- College graduates with degrees in their job area
- Professionals like engineers, MBAs, physicians, lawyers
- People with advanced degrees in other disciplines like history, math, fine arts
- Customers whose educational backgrounds are varied, and you don't have a clue about how varied they might be

If you don't factor in the educational backgrounds of your readers, you'll miss getting your message across. If you have a message going to both accountants and financial managers, for example, you may have to include some information for one group that others don't need. Sometimes, you will want to compose two separate messages, one for each group of readers.

Work and Life experiences of your audience—The newly graduated engineer may have the same educational background as his project manager but lack extensive day-to-day experience on the job. Perhaps a new engineer doesn't have experience with the company culture. You must take these two factors into consideration when you get ready to write. Obviously, you wouldn't compose a message to the engineering staff explaining terms and ideas that are old hat to the other two hundred readers just so the new engineer would understand it. But, if a significant number of your readers have little work and company experience, you should consider their relative inexperience as you write. If you are a personnel manager writing to explain company policy on sexual harassment to a group of newly appointed managers, you must account for their relative inexperience as well as their gender. The same message to an experienced group of managers who have been through a company training program on sexual harassment would probably be much different.

Other not-so-obvious factors may influence how you consider your audience. How about writing to employees during a time of labor unrest? The AFL-CIO once sent some representatives to the Digital Equipment Corporation plant where I worked to convince employees to start the process of certifying a union. Because I was a manager at Digital at the time, I got memos telling me how to answer questions people in my group might ask. Those memos were very specific about what and what not to say and do because their purpose was to help management avoid illegal or counterproductive actions. The employees who were targets for the union action, on the other hand, got memos countering the arguments put forth by the union and listing the benefits of not belonging to a union. These memos were designed to remind employees of present benefits that might be lost in a union shop.

If you work for a company with an international work force, you will have to consider the cultural differences of your readers as you work out your memo or letter. I once helped write and produce a training videotape for field engineers in Digital's international customer service force. Because the role we had assigned to a woman in the videotape was unacceptable for some foreign audiences, we had to modify parts of the videotape. Because I had not thought of that cultural aspect of my varied audience, my boss wasn't very happy with me. I had tried to show the equal opportunity nature of our company, but hadn't considered other cultural aspects. Although you won't be faced with extremely varied audiences every time you write, you must be aware that these possibilities exist and account for them.

Reader attitudes toward your purpose—If anything about your audience is absolutely critical, it is this fact: writing to a hostile audience requires a completely different approach than does writing the same message to an audience in favor of your ideas. Consider the following scenario. You are attempting to make a change in policy affecting the working conditions of all employees. Here are some possible attitudes toward the change:

• Hostile or antagonistic

• Skeptical or suspicious

• Neutral but willing to be convinced

• Friendly and sympathetic

• Eager to help make the change

How you handle this wide variation is not important at this point, but making sure that you *realize* this wide variation of attitudes as you phrase your message certainly is. This situation is one in which the "killer" in the killer rules of business communication really comes to the fore. Neglecting the attitudes of those opposed to what you are trying to do almost guarantees failure. You can "Kill" your own career with a mistake or omission here.

What are your Audience Needs?

The memory is as clear as if it happened yesterday: Paul, an engineering manager, bores a conference room full of people, including the Vice President for Engineering, for two and a half hours with the minutest technical details of a proposed project. When Paul finally finishes his presentation, the Vice President stands up, thanks him, announces that he has a plane to catch, and leaves the dumbfounded manager standing at the front of the room. Paul turns to the engineering group manager and complains, "But he didn't say if the project is approved or not." The group manager just shrugs and says, "Guess we'll have to try again next time he's out this way."

Both managers missed the point. The Vice President didn't need all the technical details of the project to approve the project. He needed first to be told that he was to approve or reject the project as a result of the presentation. Then he needed to see the resources required to accomplish the project: how many engineers, how many dollars, how much capital equipment, and for how long. He needed to know the market window, the market niche, and the probable competition. He also needed to understand the technical risks, and the confidence level of the design team in meeting the challenge of the project with the resources requested at the market window. Because the project manager didn't consider the Vice President's needs, he was completely off target with his message.

This example occurred during an oral presentation, but failures like this one occur in written presentations every day in the business world. Not considering the audience's needs is like buying a sub-compact car for a company that needs a refrigerated truck to carry tons of frozen products to customer loading docks. Although it may be less expensive, the sub-compact doesn't meet the needs of the audience. Your readers, whether they are customers or are within the company structure, need information to do their jobs or to understand how you are going to affect them and their lives. You must put yourself inside the skin of that reader and figure out what informational needs you'd have if you were the reader.

What are your Informational needs?

Informational needs are relatively easy needs to meet. What information, you must ask yourself, does my reader need to do the job or make the decision? Consider the reader's needs in each of the following examples:

- Someone who must accomplish an assigned task needs technical details.

- Managers and executives who must understand what's going on need background or overview information.

- Those making decisions at a high level need financial, resource, and timing information.

- Customers or potential customers need general information to restore or gain confidence in your product or service.

Because your audiences have such widely different needs, you may have to write more than one memo or letter. Consider the alternatives, though, if you don't take the time to get the word out. Consider a production line jerking to a halt because you didn't give some workers the information they needed. Or consider not getting approval for your project because you didn't supply the correct information to the management staff, and now your project has been shelved until next fiscal year. Or consider your customers crossing the street to a competitor because you couldn't take the time to write the message they wanted to hear. In the business world, careers are destroyed daily by such oversights.

What are your Language needs?

I teach adult writing classes for Chapman College, and at some point I usually mention that it is a good idea to write in English. The class usually laughs. They laugh even louder when I mention that although German is a perfectly good language, using German in our daily work probably won't get the job done very well. Then I ask these working adults if they have ever read instructions for a "simple, easy to use" computer program that might as well have been written in German? I usually mention a budgeting program that I bought for my computer several years ago but abandoned after several tries at making it work. The instructions were obviously written for a CPA who had a double major, the other being Computer Science. Almost every time, each class is unanimous in having had similar experiences.

I ask the students if they have become frustrated with instructions that supposedly contained the information necessary to do a job but which they couldn't find because of the language used. They all nod their heads—and understand that just writing in English isn't enough.

Knowing the educational, cultural, and technical experiences of the reader not only provides you with the information needed to accomplish your purpose, but also determines the language that your reader understands. A research chemist with a PhD may be baffled by the information written by an electrical engineer with only a bachelor's degree because the language and terms are unfamiliar. Did your parents always understand the language you used with your friends? Are business and financial terms always understood by the engineering and manufacturing staff?

If you want to communicate, you must first determine if your reader shares your working language. If so, you can use technical terms and jargon, knowing that your reader will understand. If your reader doesn't share your working language, you must:

- Explain unfamiliar terms and concepts

- Define terms and processes in simple language

- Use analogy to relate the unfamiliar to the familiar

- Use pictures and graphics as necessary to simplify

In other words, if you and your reader don't speak the same working language, you'll have to write in the reader's language, not yours. Educate your reader by explaining terms and concepts so you may use them later in your memo. Because there is no common language of the work place except simple, clear English, it is your job to make your writing communicate, not your reader's to translate it.

What does it all mean?

Marilyn Olander, a business writing consultant quoted in *The New Mexican* (Business Section, Santa Fe, N.M.: August 3, 1988, P. D 1.), said that because "Writing is one of the prime skills for business people . . . , people in management spend up to 45 percent of their time reading and writing." If she is right, and my experience says she is, you will spend, or are spending, almost half your time either reading what others have written or are writing something they will read. You will spend almost half your time in management communicating with the written word. The three keys to making sure you communicate effectively are to identify your:

• Purpose

• Audience

• Audience's needs

In the next several chapters, you'll look over my shoulder as I write several memos and a letter by looking at the purpose, audience, and audience needs for each situation. I'll use the killer rules to ensure that I produce effective communication. In later chapters, you'll watch as I use a disciplined process to write outlines, several drafts, and final copy. To end this chapter and prepare you for what we're about to do together, I'd like to quote to you from William Zinsser's *On Writing Well.* Zinsser's words are not meant to scare you but to console you.

> Writing is hard work. A clear sentence is no accident. Very few sentences come out right the first time, or even the third time. Remember this as a consolation in moments of despair. If you find that writing is hard, it's because it is hard. It's one of the hardest things that people do. (p. 12)

Chapter 2

Getting Ready to Write to the VP of Manufacturing

You stop the doodling you're doing on a legal pad and look over at Jim and Janet, who are also product managers at Kiowa Arms, Inc. Janet is looking hard at her appointment book, as if carefully studying some important detail. But the page in front of her is blank. Jim is carefully underlining words on the agenda for the meeting. He has all but two or three underlined, some several times.

Looking to the right at Bob Hollowell, the Vice President for Manufacturing, you see that he is very angry. He asks another question of Clarence McConnell, the product manager of the medical products line.

"How in the hell did your production supervisors give your assemblers the wrong procedures for that blood pressure analyzer?"

You look at Clarence out of the corner of your eye, trying hard not to be obvious, and study the effect that three minutes of chewing out have had on him.

"I gave the procedures to my supervisors in a meeting, two weeks before they went into effect. I don't know how they got them wrong."

"Did you write them down, or give them verbally," Bob says quietly, obviously trying to keep his composure.

"Verbally, sir. They weren't that hard or complicated."

"You didn't think it important enough to write them down? What

15

ever made you think they'd get everything right if you didn't write it down? What were you thinking about? Did you even bother to think?"

Clarence mumbles something that seems to die on the table in front of him. He looks in embarrassed silence at his note pad, waiting for the outburst he knows is coming his way from the almost apoplectic man at the other end of the conference room table. But the attack doesn't come.

The Vice President looks at his own note pad for a few seconds and then looks up, directly at you.

"You've got a similar problem with your phaser line."

"Yes sir. We've had a problem with the glue in the phasers deteriorating in deep space."

"I want a memo on my desk by close of business Friday outlining what you're doing about it. And it better be good. I'm in no mood for lousy communication. Don't screw it up like Clarence did, either."

"Yes sir. I'll have it Friday," you answer. "Anything special you want to know about the problem?"

"Yes. Everything! And that goes for the rest of you. The next manager to screw up like Clarence is going to get the axe."

And with that final threat, Bob Hollowell stands up abruptly, yanks open the door, and slams it behind him. The slam reverberates in the numbness in the room. Slowly the four managers in the room gather up their notes and appointment books and chance one quick look around. Nobody keeps eye contact, nobody speaks, and nobody looks at Clarence. They walk quickly to their own offices. You hurry back and sit in your office for a few minutes gathering your faculties before starting back to work.

Meanwhile, back in your office.

So, now what? As you sit there wondering about Hollowell's reaction to Clarence's mistakes, you realize you face a similar situation. You look at a desk full of papers, all having something to do with the glue problem your product line is having. You ask, "How can I possibly have all this information written up and in Hollowell's office by Friday?" Although you know you have the situation with the glue under control, you're not sure about the one with Bob Hollowell.

Let me take you off the hook for the moment. Years ago, when I was teaching young men and women to fly, one of the techniques I'd use to teach a student how to perform a new maneuver was to perform it myself and let the student watch. I'd fly the aircraft through the maneuver, describing to the student what I was doing with the controls and what visual clues I was looking for. I'd describe that I was using pressure on the stick to bank the wings to the left until the horizon cut across the windscreen at the proper angle. Then I'd say I was adding back pressure to the stick to pull the nose up and was holding that back pressure to keep the nose coming up at a certain rate until the nose got just so far above the horizon, and so forth through the maneuver.

On the second or third time through the maneuver, I'd have the student hold the stick so my movements were coordinated in the student's mind with the visual clues and my running commentary. Then I'd have the student fly the maneuver as I described what should be happening. Finally, the student would fly the maneuver without my help. I'd like to use a similar procedure here. I'll talk you through the memo to Hollowell. Follow me through by thinking carefully about what I'm doing and describing. Later, in your business career, you're on your own. I'll just be a voice in your past. I hope I'll have said the right things to you.

So, get out of your office chair and let me sit there with all those papers in front of me. Look over my shoulder. I've been faced with writing tasks like this many times and have had my share of successes with them. Let me show you how I'd handle this task and several others that you have facing you.

Start by scribbling some notes to use in writing that memo to Hollowell. That's the first step in the process of getting ready to write a memo or letter, making some notes to capture your thoughts. Because you have jotted down important facts and ideas in these notes, you can refer to them and add new ones as you outline and write your draft. That way, you won't lose good ideas or forget to include important facts. Here is a description of the problem, one that's been worrying you ever since you heard about it. (I'll include my handwritten notes used to write each section):

The glue problem.

Kiowa Arms has been producing Model 1A Phasers for Star Fleet for about three years with virtually no problems. (The Model 1A Phaser is a pistol-like weapon used by crewmembers to defend themselves against unfriendly alien creatures in deep space.) The weapons had been working perfectly until the introduction of a new teleporter on newly designed and refurbished spaceships. It seems that the new teleporters take matter apart to the atomic level rather than to the molecular level as the old teleporters did. After about 25 trips in the new teleporters the molecular structure of the glue starts to fail. Glue in one phaser failed after only 17 trips. Yet some phasers have made over 1000 trips in the old teleporters with no sign of glue failure.

— Phasers have worked okay for 3 years
    — >1000 teleportations with no problems
    — all teleporters at molecular level
— New Ships have new teleporters
    — Takes matter apart @ atomic level
    — Average failure @ 25 trips
    — one failed at only 17 trips

— Lab worked with Acme
    — New glue formula
    — 10K trips in new teleporter
    — 10X testing done — no failures

The materials laboratory has worked for several months on the problem and has developed a slightly different molecular arrangement for the glue, thereby seeming to solve the problem. Parts glued with the new glue have been teleported in the laboratory ten thousand times with no apparent weakening of the glue. After these teleportations, the lab has tested the glued joints by subjecting them to 10 times the normal structural pressures used to meet Star Fleet specifications. These tests simulate the rigors of extreme temperature, pressure, and magnetic variations found in deep space. Not one part has failed.

New gluing machines for the line.

This new glue must be applied, however, with machines different from the ones presently on the line. You'll have to order three new machines, two large and one small. One large machine will provide glue at the station (station 3) where printed circuit boards, PCBs, are laminated and have parts glued to them. The small machine will provide glue at the point on the assembly line (station 11) where all the internal components are glued to the chassis. Finally, the other large machine will be used at the final assembly point (station 15) where the chassis is glued to the case and the two halves of the case glued together.

The large machines each cost $3500 and the small one costs $2200. They are available directly from the Intergalactic Industrial Equipment Corporation. It will take one day to install all three machines, and they will be installed on 28 October 2213.

New glue needs new machines

— 3 stations on line (2 lg, 1 sm)

— Same as old stations

— Large machine @ $3500

— Small machine @ $2200

— Install on 28 OCT 2213

— Station 3 — large, PCBs

— Station 11 — small, chassis

— Station 15 — large, final assey

Note : Get model numbers from Intergalactic for purchasing

Get glue part numbers and order quantities from Acme and lab

New production processes.

Because the new machines will replace ones already on the line, there is no need to reconfigure the assembly line. The procedures are slightly different, but those differences will be covered in the training class to be held on 15 October 2213 and will be detailed in the new production procedures to be given to each supervisor for inclusion in the assembly procedures handbook issued each assembler. We'll send the production manager a memo with:

- Installation procedures for the new machines
- New gluing procedures
- New curing procedures for glued components
- Routine maintenance procedures for the new machines
- Details about the training classes

Production process

— Some line people

— Train on new machines

— Curing process is slightly longer

— Lab will train suprvs.

— Suprvs will train line

— Plant crew will install machines
    — one day
    — no special tools
    — no training needed

— Line process almost the same
    — Details of program slightly diff.
    — machine Control panel slightly diff.

  — I'll supply glue process + install proc.

      — Process
      — Procedures
      — Installation
      — Curing
      — maint. on machines

Information purchasing needs for new process.

Purchasing will need to know the models of the gluing machines to order from Intergalactic Industrial Equipment Corporation. They will also need to know the part number and order quantity of the three types of glue. The Acme Glue Products Company, Inc., is going to process glue to your lab's specifications.

Intergalactic Industrial Equipment Corp.

        IIEC Model GM — 1701 — L — 03

        IIEC Model GM — 1701 - L — 15

        IIEC Model GM — 1701 — S — 11

Note:

Call Acme @ glue #s

— Station 3

Acme GL — 1701 — 03 (12 ℓ/mo)

— Sta. 11

Acme GL — 1701 — 11 (4 ℓ/mo)

— Sta. 15

Acme GL — 1701 — 15 (18 ℓ/mo)

Base mixture

Acme BM — 1701 — 29 (30 ℓ/mo)

To clean machines and spills

Acme solvent #33 (15 ℓ/mo)

Cost information of the new gluing process

The production line is scheduled to build 10,000 phasers over the next three years. The contract with Star Fleet could be reopened for additional weapons, but for now, three years and 10,000 phasers are the planning numbers. The line has already produced 3,500 phasers, and of those, 150 have failed. You guess that another 150 will fail before you can replace them with phasers produced with the new glue. Here are some cost notes I've scribbled on a note pad:

Cost info:

- new machines
- new glue
- transportation

2 machines @ $3500 = 7000
1 machine @ 2200 = 2200

New glue adds $0.01 to each phaser
10,000 X 0.01 = $100 extra

Machines add   9200 ⎫ 10K phasers
glue adds   100 ⎭

Cost / phaser = $.93/phaser

Or repair 3.7K phasers in fleet
$20.25 each including transportation

Cost / phaser for total program = $2.44

Reduced profit from $53.74 to 51.30/phaser

No R + D costs — spread over all
deep space programs

As I look over my notes, I think I have listed everything we'll need to include in my memo to Bob Hollowell. Going through a process like this when you have to write an important piece of correspondence makes a lot of sense, and helps put the writing task into some perspective. This process puts the facts you'll need in front of you where you can see them. I find that I can *think* through facts like this while I'm exercising or driving to work. Then when I've got some paper handy, I can write them down for use as I outline and write. (I've often used a small tape recorder to capture ideas and notes as I've driven to or from work.) In many business situations, you can also get information by looking through notes from meetings, memos from others, and by phoning others for facts you don't have.

Back to Hollowell's memo (note to myself: remember, he doesn't like big words): I have information about the problem with the glue, how the problem occurred, how we are going to fix it, and how much it is going to cost. But how much of that information do I need to put in the memo to the Vice President? When Bob Hollowell said "every-thing," he was angry. What he might have said in a more calm moment is, "put in everything I need to know to make sure that this solution to our problem is really a solution and will not create another problem." He wants just enough information to feel some level of comfort with how things are being handled.

So I jot down the following questions the Vice President really wants answers to:

Hollowell wants to know —

 — what caused problem?

 — what is the fix?

 — How much trouble to line?

 — How much cost — profit margin?

 — who eats cost — us or Star Glue

— ~~what~~ when is process to start

— what is process to implement new process

What's the Purpose of this memo?

I've filled you in on the specifics of the problem on the Model 1A Phaser production line and given you my thoughts on what Hollowell will want in the memo I'll write. Now watch as I apply the killer rules to this memo. I'll start by considering my purpose in this memo. The most obvious purpose of this memo is to respond to a direct order by the Vice President for Manufacturing. He said he wants a memo with "everything" in it, and he wants it on his desk on Friday. But, besides that, what purpose or purposes does this memo serve? Here's what I came up with:

Purpose of Hollowell memo

— Let VP know things are under control

— Pass him info about
   — Problem - background
   — Solution
   — Production changes
   — Costs

& I also keep him off my back & out of my hair

& Consider absorbing cost as it is small.

Who is the Audience for this memo?

On this memo, this is an easy question to answer. The audience is Bob Hollowell.

Audience —

- *Mnd VP of manufacturing (my boss)*
- *Engineer (BSEE)*
- *MBA*
- *Very Cost conscious*
- *No marketing background*

These are the kind of facts you'll need to dig for when you write memos and letters in business. There is no reason to explain relatively simple financial terms and calculations, for example, to an engineer if he also has an MBA.

What does the Audience Need from this memo?

If I'm to satisfy Bob Hollowell and achieve my purpose, I've got to attend to his information needs. Here's a list I scratched out with what I think he'll want from this memo:

Audience needs

- *Confidence things are under control*
- *No goof like Clarence*
- *Basic understanding of problem*
- *Understand the solution*
- *Cost & scheduling info*
- *Hit on bottom line $*

— make him feel good — positive side of fix to problem

I threw in that last item, even though Bob Hollowell might not have put that one on a list if I'd have asked him for it. One of the most important strategies of successful communication is to present material in a more positive light. People are more receptive when there is something upbeat in the correspondence they receive. Bob seemed pretty angry about the bad news he got from Clarence, so let's not hide any good news from him.

Using the *Purpose, Audience,* and *Audience Needs* we've just looked at, here's the outline I came up with:

I. Background information on problem
    A. Old glue
        Old vs new teleporter
        @ molecular level > 1000 trips without failure
        @ atomic level < 25 trips before failure
        Changed molecular structure
        Extreme temperature and pressure changes
    B. New Glue
        Resists molecular changes
        10×10^3 trips in tests without molecular change
        $10 \times$ normal tests without failure
II. New Procedures Needed
    A. Installation of new machines
        Two large and one small machines
            One large machine at PCB lamination and assembly
            Small machine at chassis assembly
            Other large machine at final assembly
            One day to install and test new machines
        Cost and schedule of cutover to new process
            Large machines cost $3500 each
            Small machine costs $2200
            Cutover on 1 November 2213

   B. Production changes

       Machines replace old ones at same stations

       New procedures essentially the same

       Curing process is slightly longer than old process

       One training class for all assemblers on 15 October 2213

   C. Communicating installation and production changes in memo covering:

       Installation procedures

       Gluing procedures—to be included in production process book

       Curing procedures—in process book

       Machine routine maintenance—in process book

       Details of training class

   D. Communicating with purchasing

       Purchase three new machines and spare parts

       Purchase three new type of glue

       Rates for reordering glues

III. Effect on Profit of product line in future

   A. Cost over production run—10 K phasers over next 3 years

       Machines add $0.92 per unit

       Glue adds $0.01 per unit

       Labor costs remain the same

   B. Cost to repair 3.7 K phasers already in fleet

       150 failed phasers @ $50.37 per unit

       150 expected failures before replacement @ $50.37 per unit

       3.4 K phasers repaired @ 500 per month schedule @ $20.25/unit

   C. Overall

       Reduces expected profit from $53.74/unit to $51.30 per unit

       R & D costs can be absorbed by other product lines

IV. Recommendations for handling Star Fleet Headquarters on fix

   A. Considerations

       Phasers met specs with old glue

       Star Fleet changed teleporters without changing specs

       We could force them to pay for fix

   B. Recommendations

       Recommend we absorb cost as good will gesture

         Cost doesn't affect profit too badly

         New glue process good on other new products

> Good will and new glue could give us a competitive edge in additional phaser buys
>
> Inform Star Fleet immediately of new glue, dates, and cost

As you can see, the outline is pretty detailed and covers much of the information I came up with in my brainstorming. Given the anger the Vice President displayed toward Clarence's goof, I surely don't want to send him a memo that doesn't meet his expectations. I could be teleported into deep space and held together by some inferior glue.

Where to go from here?

I should now be ready to write the memo to the Vice President. I've brainstormed to come up with as many ideas and details as possible. Any information I needed but didn't have at my fingertips I can get from other memos or people I work with. Doing my own brainstorming, however, allows me to come up with a list of information I already know and discover what I need to find out. Remember, you can brainstorm even when you're not at your desk. Do it in the shower, while driving to work, or while exercising.

Although I would probably start writing the memo to Hollowell as soon as the outline was finished, I'll put it off for a while and work on the outline for the production manager. I'll do that right away so you can see how a different purpose, audience, and audience needs change the way I present some of the same information. Because some of this information will *not* appear in the next memo, watch for the changes. Look over my shoulder again, and follow me through the process to get an outline written for the memo to the Production Manager.

Chapter 3

Getting Ready to Write to the Production Manager

You LOOK UP from the memo you're writing as Steve Berg, the production manager on the Phaser line, walks into the office. He is there to get more information about the new gluing process. When he brought the subject up at the manufacturing staff meeting this morning, you suggested he drop by to discuss the subject.

"Come in, Steve. Can I get you a cup of coffee?"

"No thanks. I've already had too much. Got some time to talk about that new gluing process?"

"Sure. I'm just finishing a memo to Bob Hollowell on that very subject."

Steve looks around as if guilty of something and lowers his voice. "Bob sure looked at you in a funny way when I asked about procedures for the new process. What was that all about?"

"It's a long story, Steve. Not one for young ears like yours."

Although Steve is one of the youngest production managers in the corporation, he is also one of the best. You don't want to let on about Clarence, so you use Steve's age as a subtle way to avoid the topic.

"Don't worry about the new process, Steve. You'll be getting three new machines. They'll go where the glue machines you have now are. The process is virtually the same, except the curing time is a bit longer."

"Then there won't be any fewer people on the line or tasks for each station?"

"That's right, Steve. Everything's about the same."

"Good. The rumor mill is starting to get cranked up, and I'd like to stop that before it gets out of hand."

"Good idea. As soon as I finish this memo to Bob, I'm going to start on one to you. It will have the information you'll need to get the cutover to the new process done quickly."

"How about the process books? Are there any changes for us to make to them?"

"I've asked Stan Lavalle to get the R & D lab and the company that makes the new glue machines to work out those process changes for us. Although Stan is a new manufacturing engineer, he's got lots of experience in process design and should come up with a nice package for you."

"Sounds like all I could ask for."

"We try to make it easy. The memo I'm sending you will have some overall info, the installation procedures, and the procedures for the line. It should be done in a couple of days. As soon as Stan gets the process steps to me, I'll include them as a tear out from the memo to copy and put in the process books."

"Thanks. I feel a lot better about this knowing I won't have to make drastic changes on the line. Those folks are good, but change makes them nervous. And when they're nervous, I'm nervous."

Steve walks from the office looking much happier than when he came in. You, however, mumble something about always having to worry about getting people to change, even when it is obvious the change is important and in everybody's best interest. You make a note to remember to include something in the memo to Steve about the minor nature of the changes in the new process.

What is my purpose in this memo?

Here we go again. The conversation with Berg should help me determine the purpose of the memo as I start to brainstorm for it. Here are my notes:

Memo to Production

Purpose

- for production mgr & staff
- provide installation procedure
- provide new gluing process
- provide machine maintenance instructions
- have new pages or processes for production books
- give production costs
- Any relevant management info.

Each of the items listed is a family of items I must sift through, discarding those with no relevance to Steve's line and including those he and his people need to do their jobs. I must now think through these topics, trying to pin down my purpose. At this point, here's a short statement of my purpose.

My purpose is to provide the production manager clear, accurate instructions he can use to get the new machines installed and the new process established. Additionally, I must try to allay any fears on the part of the production people about changes made because of the new process.

As I consider my audience and my audience's needs, however, I may have to come back to this purpose statement and revise it. For example, I may find that my audience needs information that falls outside the scope of my purpose statement. If that's the case, I'll need to reconsider my purpose and change it to reflect what I've discovered about my audience.

Who is the audience for this memo?

Just as with the memo to Bob Hollowell, it's pretty easy to pick out
the audience for this memo; it's Steve Berg, manager of the phaser
production line. But is Steve the only audience? Don't I have other
audiences to consider if I'm going to give Steve the exact procedures
I want his people to follow during installation, gluing, curing, and
machine operation? And how about others on Steve's staff who will
oversee parts of the changes to machines and processes?

It's been my experience that office correspondence meant for one
audience often gets disseminated within the group and to the levels
immediately above and below the original audience. You must consider that fact when you write. In most cases, however, it it not your
job to write so someone other than your intended reader clearly
understands your message. Suppose you send a memo about financial
information to a manager, and she shares it with a staff member who
has little financial background, say a personnel specialist. That personnel specialist is not your intended audience and may have difficulty
understanding complex financial data and terminology. That's not
your fault.

But, if you know that the memo you send might get sent to that
manager's staff for action, then you had better write it in language
the staff can understand. In the case above, suppose the memo stated
that the other manager must staff and train for a new financial system
the company will be implementing within six months. Now, because
you must communicate those facts and their implications, you must
also write to that personnel specialist so he can take the necessary
steps to recruit, hire, and train people to support the new system. If
you want to be an effective communicator, you must look beyond the
obvious when considering your audience. Anticipate how your letter
or memo will be used, and consider the wider audience as appropriate.

So as I brainstormed and made notes about this memo and its
audience, I came up with these audiences I'll have to deal with:

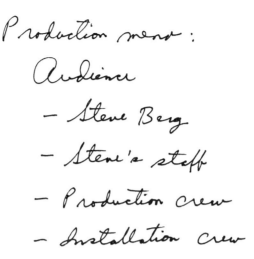

Production mem:
Audience
— Steve Berg
— Steve's staff
— Production crew
— Installation crew

Four different sets of people will use the information and procedures I'll write. Let me elaborate a bit about this varied audience:

- The first is obviously Steve Berg, the manager who will implement the changes.

- Next, there's Steve's staff who will direct and oversee the changes.

- Then, the technicians who need directions and instructions for installing and checking out the new machines on the line.

- Finally, the production workers, the assemblers, who need clear and accurate instructions for using the new machines, gluing the phaser parts together, and operating the gluing machines as a part of their daily work.

Confusing? Don't worry; just start thinking this way. With practice you'll soon handle audience variety as second nature. When Clarence didn't, you saw what Bob Hollowell thought. Remember that fully half of your time as a manager will be spent communicating with other people in your business. Some managers only make *attempts* to communicate because they don't take the time to size up their audience. Don't make that mistake.

What does this varied audience need from this memo?

With all this as background, I'll brainstorm my audience's needs with the four sets of readers in mind. Remember, I'll be providing essentially the same information to all the people I write to about the new gluing procedure, but I'll leave out some information for one audience and include other information for other audiences. I'll also put different emphasis on the information as the context for the information changes. So, using the information I came up with while brainstorming, here's what I think Steve Berg and his supervisors will need from this memo:

Production memo

Audience needs

- Management info
  - schedules
  - training
  - Cost
  - personnel – no layoffs

- Installation procedure
  - where
  - when – tools
  - how – AC power
          – use Intergalactic manual
          – 3 station
          – steps for each station

- New gluing process – 3 station
                       – steps for each station
                       – no new people
                       – no layoffs

- New Curing process
  - no new ovens
  - a bit longer

- machine maintenance
  - Use Acme solvent
  - Use Intergalactic manual

- Training for new process
  - Lab trains supvrs.
  - Supvrs train line personnel

That's a pretty long list of items to include in the memo to Steve, but I also need to include information for the installation crew. Here's a shorter list for those folks:

Installation crew needs

- Tools – nothing special

- Procedures – from manual

- Stations on the line

- Any special handling

- Checkout procedures – from manual

This list is shorter because the installers need information about only one phase of the switch to the new machines and procedure. If I add extraneous information about the gluing process or the curing process, I might confuse the installation crew. You must be careful to include only the information necessary for the reader to do the task at hand. Especially critical when you are directing someone to perform exact procedures, too much information can cause confusion for the person trying to perform a procedure.

Several years ago I wrote a user manual and a reference manual to go with a software package that let personal computers communicate with other computers. When I asked who the audience was for the manuals and software, I was told the target user was a non-technical person who used a personal computer in business. Imagine my concern when I discovered that the earlier manuals contained over five hundred pages of detailed technical information. All the procedures the user needed were in those five hundred pages but were buried in extraneous technical detail.

I wrote a 20 page tutorial that contained all the information necessary to allow the user to install the software on the computer, insert the telephone numbers and characteristics of the computers that would be called, and call the company computer to see how easy the procedure was. Then I pulled out the commonly used advanced procedures the user would want after becoming familiar with the basic program and put them into an easy-to-use format. When I finished, I had pared about five hundred pages of complicated technical data down to less than one hundred pages of clear procedures. The earlier manuals had been written by engineers who had not considered who would read them. If those manuals had gone out with the product, very few of the users would have been able to make their computers operate properly. Imagine the lost sales and returned programs.

Back to writing this memo, though. Here is the list of informational needs I've come up with for the assemblers on the line:

Needs for Assemblers

— Operation of machines
— start of day
— putting in glue
— Cleaning

— Process on line
— parts loading — for each station
— sequence of operations

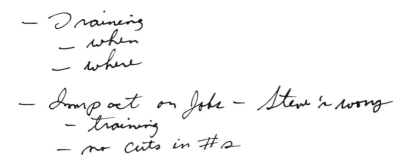

I added the last item because of the comments Steve made. He obviously needs to provide a "job security" message to his workers, and it will be more credible coming from you, Steve's manager. Consider the audience and the audience's needs, always!

The audience must immediately understand a memo's purpose.

When I started the memo to Bob Hollowell, I knew that he would know the purpose of that memo. Because he asked for it, he'll know its context. This memo, however, is different. You must let your reader know the purpose of everything you write, right up front. Let me give you an example of what can happen when you don't let your reader in on your purpose right away. Fifteen years ago I was stationed at the Pentagon and would arrive each day to an in basket overflowing with memos. It was a depressing sight because so few of those memos were well written.

Here's how I'd start each morning: I'd pick up the first memo, glance at its subject line, and then start to read. More often than not, by the time I got through the first five or six pages, I'd set the memo down on a pile I called "things I'll read later when I have more time." I'd pick up the second memo, usually another long one, and after reading about a half page, add it to the stack to read later. After five or six memos, I'd usually come to one that clearly stated its purpose in the first or second paragraph. As soon as I knew the purpose of the memo, I could decide whether or not I had to read it. Many memos get circulated to people who don't need the information or need to act on it.

If I had a dozen memos in my in basket, by the time I got to the bottom, I'd probably have put ten in the stack of memos to read later. Why did I put them into that pile? Because I was too busy to read all five or six or ten pages only to find out that I didn't need the information in the memo. Later, I learned that many memos had their purpose hidden in the final paragraph. When I learned that, my procedure varied slightly. I'd read the first paragraph or two and then the last one before throwing a memo on the pile of "things to do if I find the time." Would it surprise you to learn that I usually didn't find the time to read that pile? You'd probably laugh if I told you that when the pile got too large, I'd move it from my desk to the green circular file the janitors emptied every night? You wouldn't laugh, however, if one of those memos was yours and you wanted me to act on it.

So how can you ensure that your reader will read and act on your correspondence when necessary? By using a simple and obvious idea. Put your purpose in the first paragraph of any memo or letter you send. Even if you have to be as obvious as saying, "The purpose of this memo is. . . ," your reader at least won't throw your memo into the pile that doesn't get read. If a reader isn't one who must act on what you've asked, she can pass it on to the correct person. If a reader isn't involved in that activity at all, he can throw the memo directly into the green circular file and not clutter his desk. And you can be sure your target audience will know your purpose immediately.

Another result of clearly stating your memo's purpose up front is that your reader will have a context for the information in it. Have you ever read a letter you received from your insurance company, a state agency, or a federal agency and wondered why you were reading it? Usually, you guess at the purpose of the letter, only to be surprised somewhere near the end. Then, you have to read the letter again, this time with the real purpose in mind. Maddening, isn't it? How often do you swear under your breath and throw the letter away before you finish it? I have. And everyone else has too.

So, I want to be sure to start my memo to Steve Berg with a clear statement of its purpose. You can even give the title "Purpose" to your first paragraph to call your reader's attention to it. Many companies and government agencies have adopted this formal device so writers will at least put their purpose at the beginning. Just because a paragraph is titled *Purpose,* however, doesn't guarantee that the writer will provide it. Sometimes that paragraph is written before the writer discovers his real purpose, which often happens near the end of the memo. Then the stated purpose and the real purpose are different, much to the reader's dismay.

What does my outline look like?

I'll first show you the original outline I developed for the memo to Steve Berg and then show you how I modified it and why. Here's the original outline (I'll copy it electronically into this file. I'll discuss writing with a computer or word processor in a later chapter):

I. Purpose of memo
   A. Procedures
   B. Training
II. Procedures
   A. Installation procedures
   B. Gluing procedures
   C. Machine operation procedures
III. Schedule and resources
   A. Training
   B. Installation
   C. Cutover for new procedure (Cutover is the time when the new procedure replaces the old one.)
   D. Personnel
   E. Cost per unit

Notice that I put my purpose first and decided that my purpose had two major topics, procedures and training. As I thought more about the structure of the memo and my three audiences, I considered how Berg will use the memo. He will probably photocopy the procedures for installation and production, and distribute them to the people who need them. Considering those facts, I should restructure the memo slightly to help that process. If I put all the information Steve and his supervisors need at the front of the memo and the procedures for the installation and production crews at the back of the memo, then Steve can direct his groups to the appropriate part of the memo or photocopy sections of it to use more efficiently. This structure will also make sure that Steve and his staff don't stop reading when they come to the procedures section in the memo and miss some of the other management information provided later.

So I restructured the outline slightly, putting all the management information up front followed by the installation procedures and gluing procedures. Here's what it looks like now:

I.   Purpose of memo
     A. Procedures
     B. Training
II. Schedule of resources
     A. Training
     B. Installation
     C. Cutover for new procedure
     D. Personnel
     E. Cost per unit
III. Installation procedures
IV. Gluing procedures
     A. Training
     B. Cutover for new procedure
     C. Personnel
     D. Glue procedures
     E. Curing procedures
V.   Machine operation procedures

Notice that I've repeated some of the management information in the part of the memo dealing with gluing procedures. I added that after considering Berg's remarks about his people's concerns. I'll repeat the information in their part of the memo, so they'll have something to help overcome their reluctance to change.

So, now my initial work on the memo to the production department is complete. I've looked at my purpose, audience, and audience needs. I've considered that my audience is varied and has different needs, depending on each person's position in the production department. Additionally, I've tried to address some of Steve Berg's concerns in my planning. I'm now ready to start working on the first draft of this memo.

Chapter 4

Writing the First Draft

GETTING STARTED is hard. I'll not deny that, nor will anyone else with any kind of writing experience. Even though I've been writing business correspondence for thirty years, I still find it hard. Each chapter of this book, for example, has seemed like something I'd be better able to handle tomorrow. I've found more errands to run, more chores to do, and more conversations to have with my family than you can imagine. Knowing that I have to get this book done, however, forces me to discipline myself. I'm using the process I'm outlining for you in this book. Here are some other tricks I've learned over the years. Some I've discovered on my own; others, students and writers have shown me.

Write a non-stop draft.

Have you noticed that any time you start writing and get the first paragraph or two done, the rest goes a lot easier? Writing is never as scary when faced as it is when imagined. So, take advantage of that idea and write what I call a non-stop draft. Once you start writing on a section of the outline, don't stop until that section is done. When you start writing a memo, letter, or procedure, *keep writing*. Don't stop to check a word you think you've spelled wrong. Don't stop to work out the grammatical details of a sentence that seems wrong.

Don't stop to check facts and figures (if you're doubtful, make a note to yourself in the margin). Don't stare at a sentence you've written to try to figure out its punctuation. Don't stop, period.

Why? Because your brain works in an associative way. One idea drags forth another, and it drags forth a third. These ideas flow from the brain, down the arm, and out the pencil onto the paper. If you stop to check spelling or a grammatical point in the first sentence, there is a real danger that ideas for the second and third sentences will never see the light of day. You've had this experience. While you're writing an essay on an exam and good ideas are flowing so quickly you can't believe it, you stop to check the spelling of a word. You spend several moments looking at the word. Then you write out several variations of the word, decide on the correct spelling, put it into the sentence, and sit back satisfied that you've just saved the paper. To your horror, you cannot remember the next point or next several points you wanted to write. Your mind has gone blank; the good ideas have vanished. When do you remember those ideas? Oh, an hour or so after you hand the exam to the teacher.

That's why I suggest that you write non-stop, so you don't lose good ideas that are working their way down from your brain to the paper. If you can't think of the right word, even though it is on the tip of your pencil, put a line or some scribbling in the sentence to mark the spot. Then go back later to figure out the word. (When I use a word processor, I type XXXXX in the space and then search for it later.) However, don't forget to check spelling and grammar later, too.

Saving the beginning until the end.

Do you remember how difficult it was to write the introduction for your high school themes? How many erasers, do you suppose, get chewed off the tops of number 2 pencils every year by high school students trying to write introductions? If you guessed at the percentage of the total time it took you to write the theme compared to the time you spent writing the introduction, what would you guess? Twenty-five percent? Thirty-five percent? Fifty percent? It was a lot, wasn't it? Why do you suppose that is?

The introduction to a piece of writing tells what the writing is about, doesn't it? When you start writing something, do you really know what it's about? Probably not. You discover that as you write. How easy did the conclusion seem, compared to the introduction? A piece of cake, you say. Sure it was, simply because you know what you've written about. You've finished writing it. So, one technique I suggest is to write the introduction after you've written the rest of a memo or letter. You might write your conclusion, move it up as an introduction, then write another conclusion. After all, the introduction and conclusion both show what the writing is about, although usually in different ways. Then rewrite both sections, one to lead in, the other to point back.

Where is it written that you must start writing at the beginning of a memo or letter? I don't remember seeing that anywhere. Look over your outline. Is there something that appears easy for you to write? Then write that part first, getting yourself started and filling the blankness of the paper or screen in front of you.

Start with the hardest part.

If you'd rather save the easy parts till last, pick one of the tougher parts you'll have to write and start there. Why? Because doing so makes finishing a project so much easier. If you pick the toughest job to do first, you'll find that anything becomes easier as you move along. Here's an example—not from writing, but from life. In 1968 I was flying a small observation airplane in Vietnam and had to fly into five special forces camps located in remote mountain valleys. Because these camps had very short, dirt runways hacked out of the jungle, only the smallest airplanes could use them. The longest runway of the five was 1200 feet and the shortest 800 feet. The surfaces of these runways would test the ruggedness of a good four-wheel drive vehicle. The first time I had to go out to the camps I was terrified about landing at them, so I decided that I'd try the 800 foot strip first. If I made it into that strip, I could probably make it into the others. When I made that one, I tried a 1000 foot strip next. When that was safely behind me, the rest were easy.

I often use this approach to writing, too. I often start with the hardest part to make the rest seem easy. This approach works best for those writing tasks I really don't want to tackle. Having the hard part behind me makes the task seem more manageable. Remember that getting started is the key. Where and how you start depends on your perception of the job ahead.

Start with a section you have all the information for.

It's not uncommon in business writing, particularly with longer letters, memos, and reports, to have to start writing before all the facts are available. If that's the case, start with a section for which you do have all the facts. Keep writing until you run out of material. If you write each remaining section as the facts become available, you'll have the piece written shortly after the last fact shows up on your desk. This procedure will break up the writing into smaller chunks and make it seem less burdensome. It will also help you avoid a panicked session to get the piece written after all the information becomes available. Don't use the excuse "I can't get started yet because I don't have *all* the facts."

Or write one section and then revise it.

Another process I'm going to describe works for many writers, but it's not for me, so I give it to you as an alternative to consider. William Zinsser, in his book *On Writing Well,* a classic on writing non-fiction articles, says he cannot move to a second paragraph until he has revised the first to his satisfaction. If this process works for you, use it. I should mention several points, however. I find it hard to revise when I'm not sure where the rest of the document I'm writing is going. Just as I find it hard to write an introduction first, I find it hard to revise as I'm going along. You may lose some of the ideas that flow in a continuous stream once you start the writing process, ideas I spoke of earlier, that fly away only to be remembered after you mail the letter.

If you find non-stop writing a bit difficult, however, then try using the paragraph by paragraph approach. Write a paragraph or a section non-stop, revise it to your satisfaction, and move on to the next paragraph or section. Continue this process until you've covered the entire outline and your first draft is finished. In any method you choose, though, stick to the outline and don't deviate from it. Using an outline is one key to successful business writing.

Let your first draft cool.

When most writers finish the first draft, their first inclination is to "clean it up." We want to find and correct spelling, grammar problems, and punctuation. That's a normal, but incorrect, feeling. Because the words, ideas, and phrasing in that paper are so immediate in your mind and seem so unalterable, you will not readily see the problems. You'll skip over errors without seeing them. A sentence that is garbled will seem unfixable. The way you phrased it the first time seems to be the *only* way to say that idea. Given time, however, the faults will jump off the page at you. Don't you remember those school or college themes you wrote that seemed perfect until you looked at them two minutes before you had to hand them in? You suddenly saw misspelled words, words you left out, and poor phrasing. Alas, it was too late then to do anything about it.

If you are writing a *long* letter or memo or an especially important one, give yourself at least one day before you revise it. A delay will allow the document to cool so you can be objective about it. When you come to the document with a fresh mind, you will see the grammatical errors, poor phrasing, and technical inaccuracies. Those words that seemed "awesome" at first glance look "awful" the next day, for instance. Use time as your ally. If you start early enough on that first draft, you'll have the time to revise it properly.

When you have a *short* memo or letter to write, you can use other techniques to help get some intellectual distance from the first draft. I'll often write several memos from about 9:30 to 11:00 in the morning. Then I go to the locker room, suit up, and work out. The workout clears my mind of what I've written that morning. When I come back, I revise the first drafts while eating my lunch at my desk. If you find you write best in the morning, this technique works especially well.

Or plan your writing activity for the end of the day. The drafts you finish just before you go home will be waiting for you to revise when you come to work in the morning. This technique works especially well if writing comes easier for you near the end of the day. An added benefit of this approach is that you'll feel smug about finishing a hard task just before you head home.

Another ploy is to return phone calls after finishing a draft. Because discussing other topics will give you some distance from your draft, you will come back to it fresh. Or, if you know you have a meeting at 10, write and finish a draft just before the meeting. The meeting will give you some productive time away from the draft.

Use any technique that works for you. If you use the intellectual effort and imagination you normally use finding excuses not to write that first draft, you'll find good techniques for letting the first draft cool. The idea, though, is to *let it cool*—then polish it to perfection.

Chapter 5

Computers and Business Writing

WHILE I'M LETTING my drafts (you'll see them later) for the two memos cool, let's have a little fun and talk about writing with a computer. I can imagine that some of you who are technophobes are getting ready to close the book or turn to another chapter. Don't. Please read on. I felt exactly as you do—about nine years ago. Because I had always written on a typewriter or with a pen, I thought that using a computer would unnecessarily complicate matters. Perhaps a computer would even make writing too mechanical and remove the creativity. Boy, was I wrong. The computer makes writing much easier. Let me show you why and how.

The personal computer is a fact of life in business today. Almost all businesses use them for inventory control, payroll, accounts payable and receivable, training, filling orders, writing letters, writing books, for almost any writing that people did by hand before computers came along.

So, regardless of what business you are or plan to be in, the chances are that you will have access to a personal computer. Why not find out how it can take some of the pain out of writing and help make you a better writer? Because the computer is just a bunch of electronic components, it will only do what you tell it to do. You have to be smarter than the computer, but that's not very hard because computers are basically very dumb. Let's look at how your personal computer might help you write.

The stuff you can see and feel—Hardware

When you hear people talk about hardware and software, they'll often throw around a bunch of acronyms and terms that leave you with a feeling that there is too much to learn to be able to use a computer. Don't believe it. The computers and programs today in the business world are easy to learn and exciting to use. Here's a short rundown of some of the pieces of equipment you'll have available.

First, of course, is the computer sitting there on your desk which for obvious reasons is commonly called a desktop computer. Earlier I referred to it as a personal computer. That term was used for several years to distinguish it from the larger computers used by groups of people. Those larger ones are still around, and desktop computers are often connected to them, allowing a person using a desktop computer to get information or to do some operation that is easier for the larger one to do. The most common of desktop business computers are the IBM compatible computers and the Apple Macintosh. There are some others, but these seem to be the most common and the ones you'll likely have on your desk.

A new kind of computer is starting to show up in large numbers in the business world, the laptop or portable computer. The portable computer has been around for a while, but, except for some specific uses, has not been very popular. Because many people who have to travel frequently have come to depend on their desktop computers, the laptop is starting to become popular. Strictly speaking, the laptop is a special category of the portable computer. The portable computer is one designed to fold up into a package the size of a large briefcase, allowing the user to haul it around. The laptop is a portable designed to be small and light enough to sit comfortably on a person's lap while in an airliner or in a hotel room. Portables are often a bit too large and heavy to hold on your lap for any period over about five minutes. After that time you'll need help standing up again. These portables and laptops have the capacity to run the same programs as desktops. They usually are a bit slower, though, and have screens that are harder to read. Because they work fine as substitutes for the desktop computer, many people take the laptop back and forth from the home to the office to get work done while commuting or at home.

The two other pieces of computer equipment you'll want to know about are the printer and the modem. First the printer. Most businesses now have inexpensive laser printers to produce documents that almost look typeset. The laser printer will also turn out nice crisp graphics that can be mixed with your text so you can include charts, graphs, and other illustrations in your letters, memos, and reports. These printers will directly accept the files you've written on your desktop or laptop computer. Usually, the desktop has a line going directly to the printer or to another computer which directs the activity of the printer. Some businesses use a "daisy wheel" printer for letters because they turn out a very crisp print comparable to a good electric typewriter. The major drawback of the daisy wheel printer, however, is that it will not produce graphics.

The modem is an electronic device that lets a computer use the telephone to talk to other computers which are also connected to modems. You could, for example, leave your desktop computer turned on at work and call it up over the phone line from your laptop later at home or on the road. Then you could access all the files on your desktop or add files to it that you've written on your laptop. You can also call other computers that have information you need. For example, I subscribe to a database service called Knowledge Index. This service provides several dozen specialized databases in areas like finance, agriculture, religion, medicine, science, the humanities, and other diverse fields. I can do bibliograpical searches in minutes that would take hours at the library. Many businesses also have their own databases to provide immediate access to company information that might take weeks to collect and distribute.

The invisible stuff—Software Programs

The hardware I've just described needs instructions to tell it what to do and how to do it. Think of hardware as a tape player without a tape in it. It just sits there with the power light on, staring into space. The instructions that tell the desktop computer how to function are called software programs or application programs. Some of the application programs in a typical business desktop computer might be:

- Word processing programs
- Graphic or drawing programs
- Chart-making programs
- Electronic spreadsheet programs
- Database management programs
- Communications programs—let your computer use the phone
- Integrated programs having all or several of the above
- A program that manages all the other programs

Believe me, in a very short time these programs will help you more than you can imagine. They will be especially easy to use if you have a program like the last one to help you manage the others.

Why use a computer to write?

That's a good question and one I've heard a lot of writers ask. I subscribe to *Writer's Digest,* a magazine for freelance writers and aspiring writers, and that question pops up again and again. Most writers who tell about their experiences using computers to write have been very positive about their computers. Although some say they still write their outlines or their first drafts with a pencil and paper, most feel that the computer is a definite plus for the rest of the process. Others glow in their excitement about doing everything including note taking with the computer.

Here are a few of the advantages of using a computer for business writing. First, using the word processing feature of a desktop computer is very similar to using a typewriter. The biggest advantage the computer has over the typewriter, however, is that corrections and large changes are much easier to make. The "cut" and "paste" features, for example, let you "cut" a block of text from one place and "paste" it into another spot several paragraphs or pages away. This feature replaces the scissors and paste you may have used to restructure papers. Grammar checkers will call your attention to a sentence that has problems or to a sentence that isn't a sentence. And spelling checkers not only highlight misspelled words, but will also suggest several possibilities for you to choose from. Although spelling checkers usually come with large dictionaries, they also allow you to add words you may use often, your name and your company name, for example.

More advanced word processing programs even offer a thesaurus that presents you with lists of words to replace ones you don't want to overuse. Or, for example, suppose you know there is a better word than the one you've used, but you can't remember it. Because the thesaurus program will give you a list of words that are synonyms for the one you've used, you won't have to wrack your brain for the word you can't remember. Most of these programs let you select a word from the list the computer has offered and automatically replace the word in the text.

So, one of the primary advantages of using a computer to write with is that you can write more easily and quickly. You don't worry about typos as you do with a typewriter because you can find and fix them so easily. Your typing speed will increase—and paradoxically, you'll make fewer mistakes. The ease of finding and fixing problems makes people using computers better writers. They know that fixing problems is easy, much easier than asking a secretary to type a letter over again for the fifth or sixth time because of small changes in phrasing. Although the change may be needed, the hassle with the secretary may prevent the writer from making the change.

Several years ago I accepted a job as the technical writer in a division of a large computer company. Because the company made word processors, I was surprised to learn that the writers used either typewriters or pen and pencil to write their books. They handed their rough drafts to a woman who typed them into the word processor. As there were eight writers and only one word processor operator, you can guess how long the wait was to get back a word processed draft. Sometimes as much as six weeks. A year later, when I was asked to manage that group, the first thing I did was get every writer a computer terminal and had every writer using the computer as a writing tool in short order.

The writers liked having control over their documents because they could make changes as quickly as the engineers could redesign the product. They could make stylistic changes to make sentences and paragraphs read more smoothly as well as revising and editing up to the day they had to turn the document over to the typesetters. Another important fact emerged over the next two years. Although the engineering group increased three-fold in size and had a comparable increase in new projects, we were able to produce the technical documents for this three-fold increase without increasing the number of writers. Because we had such an increase in the productivity of the writing group, we had to add illustrators and editors to keep up with the writers. The writers had a significant increase in productivity while improving the quality of their writing. And they were enjoying writing more than they ever had.

How to start writing on a word processor.

I hope the example of my writing group has at least stirred your interest in learning about writing with a computer. I keep becoming more excited as newer and better programs become available. The computer removes or makes easier the dog work of writing and allows me to be more creative and communicate better. Here's one way to use those tools.

Taking Notes

You can start by writing all your notes on the computer. Start a file and type your notes into that file just as you might in a notebook or on file cards. Not only can you print out the notes to refer to them as you write, but you can also copy those notes electronically and paste them into your document as you write. If you have made a list of part numbers, for example, why retype them in your document when you can just copy them and paste them in? If you have some quoted material in your notes, you can copy it and paste that in too. With one of the newer database or hypertext programs, you can build a file of information that you can call up quickly, find a specific passage, copy it, and paste it into your document.

Creating an outline

I often brainstorm at the keyboard of my computer because I can type faster and more legibly than I can write. Then, using the notes I've generated, I can cut and paste them until I get a rough outline. I work with that rough outline, rewriting, reorganizing, rethinking, until I have a finished outline. Although the word processing program I use has an outlining feature, I don't use it because it doesn't work the way my brain does. But many other writers I've talked to love its features. It even allows writing within the outline so that you fill in the blanks and come away with a finished rough draft.

Look over my shoulder while I talk you through the outlining process I use. Try it until you work out your own process. Start with your brainstorming list, either handwritten or printed out from your computer. Type your major headings first, in the proper order for the memo or letter, leaving a space or two between each heading. Here, for instance, are the major headings of my outline for this chapter of *Writing from Scratch: For Business*.

Computers are a fact of business life
The Pros and Cons of computers for writing
How to write with a computer word processing program
Electronic mail and other network considerations

Next, expand the first major heading by looking through your brainstorming notes for second level headings. Double space the text and use the tab key to indent each entry to show the relationship of each item in the outline. (Indenting means you don't always have to remember whether you want a number or letter, lower case or capital.)

Computers ar a fact of business life
  Many business people have a computer on their desk
  Computers are often tied together
  Hardware available
  Software available
The Pros and Cons of computers for writing
How to write with a computer word processing program
Electronic mail and other network considerations

Now use the same technique to expand the second level headings with third level headings. Again, double space and indent with the tab key. Rather than using the tab key, you can move the left margin in for each level, a rather easy task on many word processors. As I worked through my outline, I decided to move "Computers are often tied together" later in the chapter, so I cut it from here and pasted it later in the outline. I changed the wording to "Communications programs" to better fit its new major topic.

Computers are a fact of business life
  Many business people have a computer on their desk
  Hardware available
    Desktop computers like MS DOS and Mac
    Laptops for traveling
    Laser printers for almost typeset quality
    Modems
  Software available
    Word processing programs
    Graphics programs
    Spreadsheet programs
    Database programs
    Communications programs
    Integrating programs having all of the above
  The Pros and Cons of computers for writing
  How to write with a computer word processing program
  Electronic mail and other network considerations

Incidentally, I created these outlines by cutting and pasting from the file with my outline in it. Why should I retype all that when I can simply cut and paste? I copied the whole outline and pasted it in each place I wanted it. Then I removed the lower level items from the first and second copies to recreate the original process. Ah, the miracle of electronics.

The first draft

Now that the outline is complete, print out a copy to work from and use it to write the first draft. If you have one of the outlining programs that lets you write within the outline, go to it. As I mentioned earlier, they don't work for me, but they do for lots of people. Try one. Maybe it will work for you. When you have your first draft finished, print out a double spaced copy. (The printed copy is often referred to as a hardcopy as opposed to the computer file which you can only read on the screen.) At this stage, don't try to work from the screen to revise your draft. You'll want to jump around from page to page, something you can't do very easily on the screen. Let the draft cool.

Revise the first draft

Take out your red pen or pencil and read completely through the hardcopy of your first draft. Check for structure, missing parts, extra parts. Draw arrows to show where to move things if necessary. Put numbers on paragraphs to show their new order. Put a big red X through material you want to delete. Make marginal notes about stuff you want to add. You can even outline the material you'll add in the margins with arrows showing where new information goes. Then fire up the computer again and call up the file of the first draft.

I'm going to recommend a process that isn't necessary to follow, but which you may want to use for a while. Call up the file of your first draft and give it a new name. For example, if you named your first draft *Memo*, rename it something like *Memo2*. You should now have two files that are identical but have different names. This procedure lets you revise and edit *Memo2* and still have *Memo* handy in case you decide later you like it, or parts of it, better. If you cut something from *Memo2* and want to put it back, you can copy it from *Memo* and paste it in *Memo2*.

Once you have *Memo2* on the screen, do all the cutting and pasting, deleting and adding, editing and rewriting you marked on your hardcopy. Do an occasional "Save" to make sure your changes are recorded in case some power failure or computer problem comes along. If you do frequent saves, you'll only lose a small bit of work when a problem hits. It's easy to get so involved with the writing process that you might forget to do frequent saves. When you have made all the changes you marked on the hardcopy of *Memo*, print out another double spaced draft. Let that cool.

Getting ready for final copy

Take the hardcopy of *Memo2* and read it. Mark it up to improve readability, grammar, and punctuation. (I'll discuss this process in a later chapter.) Use a red pen or pencil so you won't miss any of your marks as you work on the computer. Now call up *Memo2* on your computer and rename it *Memo3*, and edit it to include all your marks on the hardcopy of *Memo2*. When you have finished making your revisions, you're ready for some of the other computer aids that are available.

If you have a spell checker, run it now. Be careful. A spell checker will miss the error you make if you spell "hear" when you meant "here." You'll have to catch these errors. I make it a challenge to try to beat the spell checker by catching all my spelling errors and typos before I run the spell checker. I hope to have it find nothing. If you have a grammar checker, run *Memo3* through it, and make appropriate changes. Be careful, though, because grammar checkers only point out possible errors, not always real errors. If you're not sure about a possible error, ask someone who can help. For example, the grammar checker I use at work will often suggest that I may need a plural verb because the closest noun to it is plural. It can't figure out that the plural noun isn't the subject of the sentence.

Getting the memo or letter in final form

You should have a good document now. You've made sure of its structure, readability, grammar, punctuation, and spelling. Now you can do any final formatting and type specifications—computers let you print words and phrases in bold and italic faces—and add last minute graphics or spreadsheet information from other computer programs. When everything is ready, tell the laser printer to print the file, and walk to the printer to see what the final document looks like. Have a person in your group look over the document to catch the obvious things that have escaped your notice. Make those final changes and print a final copy to send to your audience.

Computers talking to computers

Have you ever played telephone tag with someone? You call and that person isn't there, so you leave a message for her to call you. She calls and you are out, so she leaves a message telling you she returned your call. This process can go on for days. But now, many companies have an electronic mail network that helps eliminate telephone tag. Electronic mail allows you to draft a message on your computer and send it to that other person's electronic mail box. When that person logs into the mail box, your message is waiting.

Usually, electronic mail services have a reply function that allows the other person to reply immediately to your message. For some reason, electronic mail is compelling. When I find a memo or letter in the "in" basket at my desk, I'll put it in a stack of correspondence to be dealt with when I get the chance and go on to other things. But when I log into the network and see that have mail, I immediately read it. Then, I'll reply immediately if it requires my response. Don't ask me why that happens, but everyone I know who uses electronic mail has essentially the same reaction. The message on the screen seems alive and won't let us ignore it.

I think one of the reasons we answer electronic mail so quickly is that it is so easy to reply. The computer is on. The message is in front of us. Our fingers are on the keyboard. All we have to do is give the proper commands, type our reply, and send it on its electronic way. When I worked for Digital Equipment, my boss worked 1500 miles away, several days by mail. He worked on the east coast and I worked in the Rocky Mountain area, so he was two hours ahead of me. It was not uncommon for him to have a message waiting for me when I came to work in the morning. I'd reply immediately to his message, get a return reply from him before he went to lunch, and have my reply waiting for him when he got back from lunch. If I needed to get more information to send to him, I could have it waiting for him when he got to work the next morning. We could pass information in one day that would take several weeks by mail, even express or overnight mail.

Electronic Mail that communicates effectively

Just having electronic mail, however, doesn't mean you will communicate better. It will be faster, but you can also confuse more people faster. The temptation is to draft messages quickly, answer without really thinking, and generally confuse things—all at the speed of light. So, here are a few thoughts about electronic mail messages.

First, you can only see what is on the screen, not the rest of the message that hangs off the bottom or extends beyond the top. This fact suggests that you should try to make your messages fit on one screen. Some mail systems let you scroll from the top of the document to the bottom, but not back up. If you want to see something you've already read, you have to start back at the beginning and scroll down to the item.

Sometimes, however, your message won't fit on one screen. Try to break the document up into pieces that will fit on the screen. Each piece should be self-contained, so the reader doesn't need to scroll to get to the end. Better yet, break the document into several messages, each self-contained. If you have a list of questions, your reader can reply to each one as he reads it and then move on to the next message. That also allows instant reply to those items that have quick answers and lets that other peson dig out the information and reply as the answers show up. Obviously this approach takes planning and careful drafting of your messages.

Beware of the tendency to write a quick message full of typos and ambiguous statements and questions just because you can get the mail on its way so quickly. Take the time to carefully write, revise, and edit your electronic mail so your reader doesn't have to ask questions to make out your meaning. Messages that are clear in their meaning and in the replies they ask for will get immediate attention. You'll have action and answers very quickly. Remember, you can confuse with the speed of light with a computer. A sign hanging in the cubicle of a colleague says it all: "To err is human, but it takes a computer to really foul things up."

If you have never written on a computer, don't be afraid to. The computer allows you to spend more of your limited time communicating clearly and creatively. Once you use a computer as a writing tool, you'll never want to write without one.

Chapter 6

Revising the First Draft

ENOUGH ABOUT COMPUTERS, back to the business of writing. The hard part's over. I've already finished writing two first drafts, and they've been sitting on my desk waiting for me to gather up the courage to read and revise them. The first time through each draft, I'll look at the structure of the memo to make sure all the information is in the right order, whether information is missing, and whether some information is extraneous. Here's why revision is so important.

Writing as an act of discovery.

When I tell my writing students that writing is an act of discovery, they usually agree, but their idea of discovery is different from mine. One student, for example, told me that she discovered she didn't have enough material to write the paper about abortion she wanted to write. Unfortunately, her discovery came at eleven o'clock the night before the paper was due. Another student told me he had discovered that an evil witch lives in his home computer. It destroyed his file just after he finished writing the paper and was going to print it. Although he was really kidding, he did have printer problems that wouldn't let him print the paper and bring it to class.

Those are discoveries, but not the kind I've got in mind. Have you ever tried to teach someone because you felt you had enough experience in the subject to teach it? Things go along just fine for a while, and then the novice asks you a fairly simple question, one you should know the answer to. But you have never really considered the question from the angle your student asked it. Remember how hard it was to come up with the answer? You learned a lot about that subject as a result of that question, didn't you?

Writing's a lot like questioning. The notes and lists you make while brainstorming are only random ideas. As you structure those notes and lists to make an outline, you create a tentative structure. Although you have learned something about your material, it's only a beginning. Real learning occurs when you write about your thoughts and hang them on your outline. New ideas creep into your mind, and new relationships between the "facts" of your material suddenly appear.

Is the structure right?

You have learned more about your material as you have written. Ideas that seemed simple suddenly take on a complexity you never guessed at. Those ideas that just wouldn't fit suddenly become some simple patterns that make you wonder how you could have been so stupid as to not have seen them earlier. You have fashioned new structures and relationships between the materials of your writing. But those structures and relationships were not present at the beginning of your writing. Nor were they all there at the middle of your effort. No, they became complete, if indeed they ever become complete, as you finished writing your first draft. Therefore, the first step in the revision process is to make sure the organization of your draft still achieves your purpose.

Let me give you an example that is happening to me right now. As I write this paragraph, which I'm adding to this chapter as I'm revising it, I'm in the midst of restructuring the whole book. Not only did this chapter that started life as chapter 9 become chapter 6, but this is the third chapter that has been chapter 6. Although the material in this book is very familiar to me, I'm learning more about it as I put it into a structure that works properly. I've seen, as I've written, that you will learn more easily if I put chapters in a slightly different order. If I left this chapter where it was, you would have waited too long to see how to revise the first draft. That fact was not apparent to me until I saw how much material came between writing the first draft and revising it.

Is everything there that should be there?

Perhaps you have even discovered some ideas you've left out, because you didn't know them, or had forgotten them, when you made your outline. One benefit of the process I'm showing you in this book is that you'll allow yourself time to make major adjustments like this one. Suppose you are writing at midnight the night before the paper's due (or at one o'clock in the afternoon and the memo is to be on your boss's desk at two) and you find you've left out material. If you know the material, you aren't in too much trouble, but suppose you need to do some research to find the facts you need?

Often, you will find that you need to do more research because either the information you thought would work looks weak on the page, or the facts seem not to support a conclusion you've reached. If you have allowed enough time, you can do that extra research, make a few phone calls, or look back through notes you've made at meetings or conferences.

Several months ago I drafted a fairly extensive plan for a set of technical manuals and training courses for a software product one of my clients was designing. I felt good about the plan because it was the most comprehensive one ever written for the writing group. Because I was a consultant to the group, I wanted everything to be right—an extension of my contract was in my mind, of course. Each time I read over the plan, it seemed that something was missing. Although I had spent a lot of time researching and discussing the details, and I had learned a lot about the operation of that software group and of the new product we were to document, something was definitely wrong.

I was talking to one of the company's staff writers about his project when the missing piece suddenly fell into place. I had mentioned the need for three or four contract writers. I had mentioned the need for "hands-on" time at an engineering design workstation for writers and course developers so they could learn the new software. I had mentioned the need for time to train new contractors who would document the new product. What I had neglected to mention, however, is that we'd need at least three new desktop computers with word processing software for those contractors to write on. Luckily I had time to add them to the draft document before we had to review it at a design review where we would get approval for the resources we'd need.

So, give yourself the time, as I've advocated throughout this book, to let your draft cook and stew in your subconscious. If you listen to that little voice that says you have a problem, you'll be surprised at how often that little voice is right. Good decision-making is often based on immersing yourself in facts and letting those facts suggest a solution to a problem, even if the solution is not a traditional one. That your intuition can often provide help is significant—because there are few absolutes in writing. Let your "little voice" help you to some great solutions to writing problems.

So, if you've discovered that you haven't covered something in enough detail or have left something important entirely out of your draft, now's the time to add it. Adding a new piece may mean that you have to reconsider your structure again. Should the new piece go up front, or near the end? Is it a part of some piece that's already there? Or does it become a major part with something already in the draft becoming a subheading to the new part? Don't be surprised if you wind up starting again from scratch. It's sometimes easier to make a new outline and produce a new draft than it is to revise a draft that is completely changed by the addition of new material.

Do you have any extra material?

The hardest task of your first revision is throwing out material you don't need. In the early chapters of this book, I discussed the need to consider your purpose, your audience, and your audience's needs. These three factors decide what does or doesn't go into a document you're writing. Too often, however, we let the fact that we've already written something cause us to retain material that we should toss aside. Because they are somehow special to us, as is our name, words we've put on paper take on some kind of magic that keeps us from throwing them away.

Once, when I was a staff officer at the Pentagon, I worked for a colonel who was a poor writer. I'll call him Weaver. His assistant, a lieutenant colonel I'll call Taylor, wasn't much better. While I was an executive secretary for a committee headed by a one-star general,

Weaver and Taylor were executive secretaries for a staff board headed by a three-star general. Our job was to sit in meetings, take notes, and write reports describing the actions taken by the generals and their associates, and to write tasking orders to staff offices as a result of these meetings. Colonels Weaver and Taylor were having trouble getting their three-star to approve their reports. As a matter of fact, he was getting rather nasty about the matter.

Since Colonel Weaver was my boss, and my reports were being approved by *my* general, he decided that I should fix his reports so that they would also be approved. It wasn't too hard to revise their reports. To paraphrase Sergeant Joe Friday, the general wanted "just the facts." Weaver and Taylor, however, were putting everything from their notes into their reports. With so much extraneous material, their reports ran to seven or eight, sometimes even a dozen or so pages.

I started by cutting redundant material; then I got rid of purely informational stuff. Because I cut out everything but the essential facts that led to decisions and tasks for staff offices, the bloated reports suddenly slimmed down to two pages consisting of one and two sentence paragraphs. The general signed the reports and said, "That's what I want from now on." Guess who got to write the reports "from now on"? Weaver and Taylor were unable to cut words they had written because they didn't have the discipline necessary to throw out the non-essential. One of the hardest things you'll have to do in your writing is to throw out sentences and paragraphs that merely show off your writing skill.

Some hints about restructuring.

There are two easy ways to restructure a document. The first method involves using more paper, a pair of scissors or a razor blade, and some paste or tape.

Once you've identified the new alignment of parts in your paper, cut your paper into chunks and position them into the new structure. If you want to add sections, type or write them and place them in their proper position relative to the ones you already have. If there are parts you want to eliminate, cut them out and set them aside, *but keep them for a while.* You may change your mind about cutting them from the final copy. Now, paste or tape the pieces you're left with onto some clean sheets of typing paper, so you have everything in the right order. What you're left with is a rather messy looking rough draft, but one that has everything where you want it. Use it to type the next draft.

If you are working on a computer or word processor, this procedure is so much easier. The section you are now reading, "Some hints about restructuring," exemplifies how easy my computer made restructuring this chapter. I had written an outline that had this section at the end of the chapter and my first draft was complete before I realized this section belonged here in the chapter rather than at the end. So, I "cut" the section from the end of the chapter and "pasted" it here. Pretty slick, isn't it?

The computer lets you add sections right on the screen without having to cut and paste the printed pages. As a matter of fact, on most word processing programs the feature you use to move pieces around in a document is called "cut and paste." That name clearly describes what you are doing, although you are doing the cutting and pasting on the screen rather than with paper, scissors, and glue. If I decide later to put this whole section, or part of it, somewhere else in this chapter, or even in some other chapter, I can cut it from this spot and paste it into the new spot electronically. And I don't get sticky fingers in the process, either.

One word of advice about doing this electronic cutting and pasting, however. Until you get comfortable with your computer program, "Copy" something you want to move rather than "Cut" it. The Copy feature leaves the original words in the document. It makes a copy that you can then "Paste" where you want it. After you've pasted the copy where you want it, you can go back and "Cut" those words from the old spot. Using "Copy" eliminates the nervousness you'll feel when you have cut a passage and are scrolling through the document to find the place in which to paste it. If you are removing passages from your document, you may want to create another file to paste those passages into. That way, if you want them later for something else or you decide you want to include them again in the original document, you've saved them so you can cut and paste them without having to write them again.

It's time now for you to look over my shoulder again as I show you how I used the processes I've been discussing first on the memo to Bob Hollowell, then the memo to Steve Berg.

How did I restructure the memo to the Vice President?

Because I bragged earlier about how I helped Colonels Weaver and Taylor get their reports signed by the general, let's see if I did as well here on the memos I'm writing. When I read through the first draft of my memo to Bob Hollowell, it was immediately apparent to me that it was longer than necessary and redundant in spots. As I mentioned earlier, I had to consider my purpose, my audience (Bob Hollowell), and Bob's needs. I think that I spent too much time on the trouble Clarence got himself into by not communicating properly, and I let myself get fooled by Hollowell's statement that he wanted "everything." Here's my original draft:

Background

Starfleet ran into problems with our Model 1A Phaser when they modified the teleporters on some of the newer fleet cruisers. The old teleporters reduced matter to the molecular level while the new teleporters reduce matter to the atomic level. Apparently reducing matter to the atomic level ~~reduces some~~ *causes* problems with matter being improperly reassembled in areas of strong magnetic fields. This new matter reduction, however, has caused problems with the glue we use in the Model 1A Phaser.

We have been using the same glues in the Model 1A Phaser for the past three years with no problems. Starfleet has phasers which have gone through over 1000 teleportations with no reduction in tensile or shear strength of the glue. With the new atomic level teleporters, however, the glue in the phasers has failed after less than 25 teleportations. This is obviously not a satisfactory performance for either Starfleet or us.

The materials lab has worked for three months to come up with a fix for the problem. The lab has designed a new glue with a base that resists molecular change during trips in the new teleporters. Testing done on the glue has shown no molecular change after 10,000 trips or when subjected to 10 times

the normal testing we've done on our products to meet Starfleet specs.
We've not had a single failure during this extended testing.

The new glue will require new glue dispensing machines at three points on
the assembly line, as well as slightly different procedures. We'll provide
training for the assemblers involved in new gluing procedures and machine
operating and maintenance procedures. The rest of this memo will provide

dup

/

you with an overview of the start up process we'll use to cut over to the new
glue and gluing process.

Installation of New Gluing Machines

We will install three new gluing machines, two large and one small one, to
replace machines already used in the phaser assembly process. These
machines will be installed at the same stations as the machines they replace,
so there will be a minimum affect on the line. The machines will be installed
as follows:

Condense & move to next section!

- One large machine at PCB lamination and assembly
- One small machine at chassis assembly
- One large machine at final assembly

We will install the machines on November 1, 2213, and will take one day to
install and test them. The cost of the new machines is:

- Large machines @ $3500   *move to financial section*
- Small machine @ $2200

Production Changes

Fortunately, there are few changes necessary to use the new glue or gluing procedure. The machines will replace older machines at the same stations on the line and the procedures are very similar to the ones now in use. There is some slight difference in the curing process for the new glue, but the changes have to do with temperature and time, not equipment or process. We will conduct a short training class on October 15, 2213, to acquaint the

2-

assemblers with the new procedures. The production supervisors will learn the new processes from the lab people who developed the glue, and the supervisors will conduct the classes.

Communicating Installation and Production Changes

I am writing a memo with appropriate attachments to my production supervisors to cover the following:

- Machine installation procedures

- New gluing procedures to be included in the assemblers' process books

- New curing process procedures to be included in the assemblers' process books

- Procedures for routine set up and maintenance of the new gluing machines

- Time, place, and details of the training class the supervisors will conduct for appropriate assemblers

Instructions for Purchasing

I m preparing a memo for purchasing to alert them for the need to buy the three new gluing machines and to order a new type of glue from Acme Glue Products Company. Inc. I'll include spare parts for the machines and order rates for the glue in that memo.

Financial Effects of New Gluing Process

3

Installing the new machines and using the new glue will have a small effect on our profit forecasts for the Model 1 A Phaser product line [Because of this small effect, I've included a recommendation as to how we may want to ~~remove~~ handle the charges to Starfleet. Those recommendations are at the end of this memo.

We Using the plan to build 10 K phasers over the next three years to complete the Model 1A Phaser contract with Starfleet as a base. here are the unit cost increases:

- New gluing machines add $0.92

- Improved glue adds   0.01

- Labor costs   0.00

We have already delivered 3.7 K phasers to Starfleet and will have to call them back to reglue them with the improved glue. One hundred and fifty phasers have already failed in service. I expect another 150 to fail before we can replace them with reglued phasers. Here are the unit costs to repair & replace the phasers already in service:

- 150 failed phasers $50.37

- 150 phasers likely to fail   50.37

- 3.4 K repaired at factory   20.25

We expect to repair the 3.4 K phasers at a rate of 1700 per month, which should get them all repaired and back in service in two months, once we start the repair cycle. We need to work the details of this cycle with

√

Starfleet. For the time being, we can increase our production rate slightly and use the excess to replace failed units from the field.

The total increased cost of the new gluing process for the Model 1A Phaser product line is:

- Cost of new machines $9,200.00

- Added cost of glue   100.00

- Repair of *existing* ~~failed~~ units   15,111.00

Total Increased Cost $24,411.00

Total per unit Cost $2.44

This will reduce the profit per unit from $53.74 to $51.30. I've not included the R & D costs in the figures because we can spread those across all our deep space product lines making the delta cost minimal.

Recommendations

The glue we have been using in the Model 1A Phasers meets all Starfleet specs and none have failed in service except with the new teleporters. ~~In effect, Starfleet has changed operating conditions without changing the specs our product must meet.~~ *remove* Our phasers, however, are failing in service and that's not good for our reputation. We could charge the additional costs we'll bear to Starfleet and be within our legal rights. ←

I'd like to recommend that we not charge Starfleet for the extra unit cost and build good will instead. The delta cost is really small and doesn't cut into our *to fix the problem* 5

profit margin very much. The glue we've developed gives us a competitive advantage we can exploit immediately on other deep space products.

My recommendation is that we notify Starfleet of the new glue, give them the data on the testing we've done ~~on the new glue~~ and tell them we'll absorb the additional cost of manufacture and ~~the cost to~~ retrofit *of* phasers already in service.

If you have any questions on the data or procedures I've outlined in this memo, please don't hesitate to call me at extension 5798.

6

You can see from my markings on the draft that I've seen the need to make major structural revisions. Some sections disappeared completely, while others needed to be condensed and moved. I'll show you some of the changes I made and tell you why I made those changes. Follow me through this discussion so you'll understand the rationale for making similar changes in your own writing.

The section entitled "Installation of New Gluing Machines" (manuscript p. 2) repeated information I'd already given in the "Background" section, and belonged in the section called "Production Changes." The next section, "Communicating Installation and Production Changes," (manuscript p. 3) seemed like overkill. Here's what the revised material looks like:

Production Changes

Fortunately, there are few changes necessary to use the new glue or gluing procedure. Three new gluing machines will replace older ones at the same stations on the line and the assembly procedures are very similar to the ones now in use. There is a slight difference in the curing process for the new glue, having to do with temperature and time, not equipment or process. We'll conduct a short training class on October 15, 2213, to acquaint the assemblers with the new procedures. The production supervisors will learn the new processes from the lab people who developed the glue, and the supervisors will conduct the classes.

I'll write a memo with appropriate attachments to Steve Berg, the production line manager covering details of training schedules, installation and production procedures, and machine maintenance.

As you can see, I've completely rearranged the material and cut a lot of detail. Why cut out so much detail? How many of the details about the gluing machines, their location, and cost does Hollowell really need? And what about telling him what I'll write to Steve Berg? Does Hollowell really need all that? Because I don't think so, I condensed and rearranged those details into two fairly small paragraphs. I also moved the sentences about the cost of the new machines to the financial section where that information belongs.

What Hollowell is most interested in are the financial details of the new process. Why did he get so upset with Clarence? The company was losing money. Vice Presidents and other top executives are usually more interested in the financial and resource implications of programs than they are in the nitty-gritty details of production and scheduling.

Notice that I cut the first paragraph, starting with "The new glue will require . . ." That material merely repeated what the next section would say, so I cut it. I got in the right mood to cut material, and I reduced redundancies, condensed the section I've already shown you, and reduced the draft from five-and-one-half double-spaced pages to slightly under four double-spaced pages. And that's only the first revision. I've revised primarily to make the structure better. Later I'll revise to make each sentence carry the right message which should shorten the memo even further. Be aware, however, that just making the memo shorter doesn't necessarily make it better. The important information *must* be in the memo, or it won't do its job.

How did I revise the memo to Steve Berg?

The memo to Steve Berg covering production changes had the following structure:

1. Management information—schedules and resources
2. Machine installation procedures
3. Production procedures
4. Curing procedures

This structure seemed logical as I did my brainstorming and outlining. However, the material in this memo looked different to me as I read through the draft. Here's the first draft with my revision marks and comments. Note that, as with the revision of the first draft to Hollowell, although I did revise some sentences for clarity, my major goal was to revise for structure.

Purpose

This memo describes production processes which will be affected by the new gluing process. Specifically, the memo will cover:

- Schedules and resources

- Installation procedures for the new machines

- The new gluing procedures   ← *New Curing Procedures*
- Machine ~~operation~~ *loading &* procedures

The sections which apply to installation procedures, the new gluing
procedures, and ~~machine operation~~ *new curing &* procedures contain the procedures to be
included in the process books at each station on the line. All ~~the~~
management information is contained in the first section.

Schedules and Resources

Because of the need to change to the new gluing procedure as soon as
possible, the schedules and resources required are tight. We must get the
line personnel trained as quickly as possible and get the new machines
installed quickly. Here are the dates and location for the key events:

- All production supervisors will be trained on the new gluing
  process on October 12, 2213. Bob Gates of R & D will conduct the
  training in the lab where the prototype machines are located.

- All assemblers associated with the gluing process will be trained in
  the new gluing procedures on Wednesday, October 15, 2213. Their
  supervisors will conduct the training. This training will also take
  place in the lab where we have prototype machines available.

- The new machines will be delivered in time to be installed on the line on Saturday, November 1, 2213. These machines will replace the three machines on the line ~~now~~ and will ~~need~~ *require* a minimum of reconfiguration of the present stations. The major difference is the location of mounting holes and brackets.

- The cut over date for the new gluing process is Monday, November 3, 2213.

The new gluing procedure will require exactly the same number of assemblers as the process you are now using, so there will be no increase in head count.

The cost per unit increases slightly with the new process, due mainly to the cost of the new machines. Since that is a capital equipment cost, it will be amortized over the next three years of production. Using an amortized cost equation, the increased costs per unit are:

- New gluing machines add $0.92

- Improved glue adds   0.01

- Labor adds   0.00

3

The cost per unit goes up to $2.44 when the cost of repairing phasers which have failed in service. The increased transportation costs account for that increase. The bottom line is that the profit per unit will slip from the currently planned $53.74 to $51.30. I've already notified Bob Hollowell of

this figure and have made recommendations about ~~whether or not to~~ recover *ing*
the increased costs.

Procedures

The following attachments . . . .

Move entire section to procedure here

4

Installation Procedure

This section contains the installation procedures to be used by the crew
which will install the three new gluing machines. I've made these
procedures self contained so you can either remove them from the memo or
copy them and give them to the installation team. Two of the machines are
large ones, replacing those at stations 3 and 15. The other is a small one to
replace the machine at station 11. The connections to electrical power are
standard and the power lines now in place will be installed on the new
machines. The largest task necessary for the installation of all three
machines is to locate new holes, drill them, install the mounting brackets,
and attach the machines to the mounting brackets. No special tools are
needed. The Installation process is as follows:

Remove to front of memo with discussion of machine.

Tools needed:

1/4 inch electric drill with 1/2 inch drill bit

Large screwdriver

Two 3/8 inch socket wrenches with 1 in sockets

Small Phillips head screwdriver

5

Unpacking the gluing machine:

You'll find

~~There should be~~ five items in each of the shipping containers

A large styrofoam cube containing the gluing machine

A smaller styrofoam box containing the mounting bracket

One plastic bag with four 1/2 inch mounting bolts and nuts

On plastic bag with twelve 1/4 inch bolts and nuts

An Installation and Operation Manual

If any parts are missing, call Henry Lancing at 5798.

Installing the mounting bracket:

1. Locate the center of the current mounting bracket and use that as
   the center of the new mounting bracket. The new bracket is

several inches larger than the old one. The open side of the new bracket should face the operator's position which is directly in front of the machine

2. Mark and drill four holes through the wood workbench area and the steel frame of the workbench.

3. Clean the drill shavings from the area and remove burrs from the wood and metal edges.

b

4. Mount the bracket with the four bolts that were provided, put the nuts on the bolts, and tighten them finger tight. You'll snug them down after the machine has been bolted to the bracket.

Mating the machine to mounting bracket

1. Lower the gluing machine into the mounting bracket so the red power switch faces the open end of the bracket. The open end of the bracket and the power switch should both face the operator station.

2. Place one 1/4 inch mounting bolt through the end hole on each leg of the mounting bracket and through the corresponding hole in the gluing machine. You should place six bolts in place. *stet*

3. Put nuts on the end of each of these bolts and tighten them finger tight. This will align the machine and ease the installation of the remaining bolts.

4. Place the remaining bolts throught the mounting bracket, place the nuts on them, and finger tighten, .\

5. Snug all 12 bolts you have just installed.

6. Now square the entire machine and mounting bracket with the workbench and tighten the four large mounting bolts. This completes the installation of the machine, .\

7

Connecting electric power to the machine

1. Make sure the circuit breaker is OFF to the lines *Power Cables* you will connect to the gluing machine.

2. Turn to page 3 of the Installation and Operation Manual that you found in the box and locate the power junction box, shown at the lower left of figure 2 and remove the cover.

3. Connect the three power leads to lugs T1, T2, and T3.

4. Connect the green ground lead to the ground lug marked GND, just below the three power lugs.

5. Replace the cover of the power junction box.

6. Place power on the machine by moving the power circuit breakers for the circuit back to ON. This completes the connection of electrical power to the machine.

Machine checkout procedure

1. Turn to page 6 of the Installation and Operation Manual that came with the machine and follow the procedure there titled "Initial Checkout and Setup."

2. Use the troubleshooting charts in chapter 5 if you encounter any difficulties. If you have problems you can't fix, call Henry Lancing at 5798.

3. When through with the procedure, turn the machine back on using the red power switch on the front of the maching. (The front of the machine faces the operator position.) Leave the machine on over the weekend to let temperatures stabilize to factory operating conditions. This concludes the entire installation process.

9

Production Gluing Procedures

The gluing procedures contained in this memo are based on all of the assemblers who work at stations 3, 11, and 15 undergoing training on them on October 15, 2213. These procedures will go into effect on the November

3, 2213. Because the procedures are so similar to the current ones, the
number of assemblers is exactly the same. The checklists below ~~provide~~ *Continue* the
procedures for each station, and the curing process all stations will use are at
the end of the station procedures. These procedures replace the ones now in
the process books for each station.

move to management section

10

Station 3 Process

This process assumes ~~that the~~ normal routing of parts to station 3 ~~will~~
~~continue~~ and ~~that the~~ normal procedures ~~will be used~~ to insert parts into the
robotic arms which present and hold the parts for gluing. It also assumes
that assemblers will use the glue loading procedures outlined at the end of
this memo.

Starting each shift

1. Turn the red power switch to ON.

2. Turn the heater switch to ON.

3. Check the heater temperature setting to 370 degrees.

4. Press the mixing switch and allow 10 minutes for proper glue
   mixing. After ten minutes, the glue machine is ready to operate.

Station 3: Gluing the PCB laminations

1. When the robot arms present the first lamination, press the #1 key on the operator panel.

2. When the robot arms present the second lamination, press the #1 key again.

3. When the laminations have been clamped by the robot arms, they will load the IC chips. Press the #2 key.

/ /

4. When the robot arm presents the power supply chip, press the #3 key.

5. When the robot arm presents the right edge connector assembly, press the #4 key.

6. When the robot arm presents the left edge connector assembly, press the #5 key.

This completes the gluing of the PCB assembly. The robot arm clamping the PCB will release the clamps and put the completed assembly into the curing holder. When the holder is full, take it to the curing oven at station 4.

12

Station 11 Process

This process assumes that the normal routing of parts to station 11 will continue and that the normal procedures will be used to insert parts into the robotic arms which present and hold the parts for gluing. It also assumes that assemblers will use the glue loading procedures outlined at the end of this memo.

Starting each shift

1. Turn the red power switch to ON.

2. Turn the heater switch to ON.

3. Check the heater temperature setting to 370 degrees.

4. Press the mixing switch and allow 10 minutes for proper glue mixing. After ten minutes, the glue machine is ready to operate.

Station 11: Gluing the Chassis Assembly

1. When the robot arms presents the PCB and chassis assembly, press the #1 key.

2. When the robot arm presents the trigger mount assembly, press the #2 key.

3. When the robot arms present the left and right multi-chip accelerator assemblies, press the #3 key.

13

4. When the robot arm presents the forward focusing ring, press the #4 key.

5. When the robot arm presents the rear focusing ring, press the #6 key.

This completes the gluing of the chassis assembly. The robot arm put the completed assembly into the curing holder. When the holder is full, take it to the curing oven at station 12.

14

Station 15 Process

This process assumes that the normal routing of parts to station 15 will continue and that the normal procedures will be used to insert parts into the robotic arms which present and hold the parts for gluing. It also assumes that assemblers will use the glue loading procedures outlined at the end of this memo.

Starting each shift

1. Turn the red power switch to ON.

2. Turn the heater switch to ON.

3. Check the heater temperature setting to 370 degrees.

4. Press the mixing switch and allow 10 minutes for proper glue mixing. After ten minutes, the glue machine is ready to operate.

Station 15: Final assembly

1. When robot arm #1 presents the lower clam-shell assembly, press the #1 key.

2. When robot arm #2 presents the trigger assembly, press the #2 key.

3. When robot arm #3 presents the lithium crystal power pack, press the #3 key.

15

4. When robot arm #2 presents the power-level adjustment switch, press the #4 key.

5. When robot arm #3 presents the upper clam-shell assembly, press the #5 key.

This completes the gluing of the final assembly. Robot arm #2 will place a clamp on the assembly and put the completed assembly into the curing holder. When the curing holder is filled, take it to the curing oven at station 16.

16

Curing Process for stations 4, 12, and 16

The curing process is the same for all three stations and is a bit longer than the old process. The ovens have not been replaced, but the curing temperature and time are different from the old ones. Use this process on all curing ovens:

At the beginning of each shift

1. Place the check thermometer into the oven and turn the oven power switch ON.

2. Set the oven temperature digital display to 1200 degrees.

3. Let the oven heat for ten minutes after the green READY light comes on.

4. Make sure the check thermometer reads 1200 degrees.

5. If the check thermometer does not read 1200 degrees, add or subtract the number of degrees from or to the 1200 to the oven temperature digital display.

6. Allow the oven to stabilize for 10 minutes after the green READY light comes on, and repeat steps 4 and 5.

   When the check thermometer reads 1200 degrees, the oven is ready for curing.

1 7

Procedures for curing parts

1. Open oven door and place one holder of glued parts into the center of the oven.

2. Close the door and press the HEAT ACCEL button.

3. Set the curing timer to 3 minutes.

4. Note that the timer starts to count down from 3 minutes when the red CURING light comes on.

5. When the red CURING light goes out, the door lock will automatically unlock. Remove the curing holder from the oven and place on the cooling bench.

NOTE: This completes the curing process. Ensure that the curing holders are not moved for at least 30 minutes after they have been placed on the cooling bench.

Add machine loading procedure

Again, follow me through as I describe the reasons for some of the changes I've made. Because of the comment Steve made about rumors of cuts in manpower on the line, I included information at the beginning of the "Production Procedures" section about training and the number of assemblers needed for the new procedures. As I looked at this material later, it was obviously out of place. Look at the revised draft (page 9) for the section entitled "Production Gluing Procedures."

When I looked again at the "Production Gluing Procedures," I realized that it belonged in the management section of the memo. These details are for the managers. It is their job, not mine, to get this information to their people. If Steve wants to photocopy parts of the memo to distribute to his supervisors and their production people, that is his decision. Putting this material where I originally put it could cause Steve and his supervisors to overlook it—it was in a section called "Procedures." The paragraph I've shown above, I lifted almost intact and dropped into the management section of the memo. I'll make changes to it on my next pass through the memo, but for now, I'm more interested in basic structure.

As I wrote out the gluing procedures, I discovered that I really needed to write instructions for each of the three stations because the procedures are different for each station, a fact that when I outlined the material did not occur to me. Here's the outline I started with:

Gluing procedures

- training

- Cutover for new procedures

- personnel

- glue procedures

- Curing procedures

When I wrote the memo, I included the first three items in this outline in the paragraph I've discussed above. Then, I realized that I had to write different procedures for each of the three stations because I had three sets and each station needed a set of curing procedures. This reorganization on the fly, so to speak, shows how you will learn about material as you write about it. Even though I saw some problems with my outline as I went along, I made other structural mistakes, such as putting the management information in the wrong place.

After I realized that moving the management information made sense, I looked back at the installation procedures and realized that I had included management information in that section, too. Here's what the first paragraph looked like in the first draft:

Installation Procedure

This section contains the installation procedures to be used by the crew which will install the three new gluing machines. I've made these procedures self-contained so you can either remove them from the memo or copy them and give them to the installation team. Two of the machines are large ones, replacing those at stations 3 and 15. The other is a small one to replace the machine at station 11. The connections to electrical power are standard and the power lines now in place will be installed on the new machines. The largest task necessary for the installation of all three machines is to locate new holes, drill them, install the mounting brackets, and attach the machines to the mounting brackets. No special tools are needed. The Installation process is as follows:

When I moved the management information up front where it belongs, the introduction to the installation procedures looked like this:

Installation Procedure

Two of the machines to install are large ones, replacing those at stations 3 and 15. The other is a small one to replace the machine at station 11. The connections to electrical power are standard and the power lines now in place will be installed on the new machines. The largest task necessary for the installation of all three machines is to locate new holes, drill them, install the mounting brackets, and attach the machines to the mounting brackets. No special tools are needed. The Installation process is as follows:

The material I removed from the procedures sections shows up in the revised draft as two paragraphs in the management information at the beginning of the memo:

Installation Procedures

The installation and checkout procedures for the new machines are simple and should require less than one day for all three machines. Two of the machines are large ones, replacing those at stations 3 and 15. The other is a small one to replace the one at station 11. I've included step-by-step instructions for installation in a separate section of this memo. The instructions are ready for you to pull from this memo, or copy, and put in the process books at each station. The installation requires no special tools, only those our facilities maintenance people carry in their toolboxes.

New Gluing Procedures

The gluing procedures contained in this memo are based on all of the assemblers who work at stations 3, 11, and 15 undergoing training on them on October 15, 2213. These procedures will go into effect on the November 3, 2213. Because the procedures are so similar to the current ones, the number of assemblers is exactly the same. The checklists attached at the end of this memo contain the procedures for each station, and the curing process all stations will use is at the end of the station procedures. These procedures replace the ones now in the process books for each station.

Although these paragraphs contain much of the same information I've included at the beginning of the procedures sections, the information is written for two different audiences. The two paragraphs included in the management section provide general information about the procedures, while the paragraphs at the beginning of the procedures sections provide more specific information for those people who have to install the equipment and glue the phasers. Here's a good example of intentionally being redundant, for a purpose. Repeating material is not a sin; repeating information *needlessly* is the sin.

You should have the idea by now how to revise a first draft to improve its structure. Before I finish this chapter, though, let me mention two more points.

Two more items to check now.

When you finish your first revision, your memo or letter should now have its final shape, its structure. But there are a few more details you should check. The first is to check that all the technical facts are accurate. Are the part numbers, phone numbers, office names, zip codes correct? Have you included the correct dates, room numbers, times? Have you spelled people's names correctly?

Let me tell you how I screwed up badly once when I didn't check a name carefully. While I was working for Digital Equipment Corporation as the manager of a technical publications group, Kenneth Olsen, the company president, made his first visit to the plant I worked in, and I was one of a few managers who was invited to lunch with him. Because the plant newsletter editor knew I was a writer, she asked me to take notes at the luncheon and write an article about it for the newsletter. I agreed and gave her the article the next day.

In large companies nothing gets printed in a company newsletter that doesn't get read by at least several high level managers. In this case the newsletter editor, two personnel managers, the plant manager, and all the secretaries in those offices read my article. I got several calls from them telling me the article was well written and informative. The newsletter editor got the go ahead and sent the camera ready copy to the printer. When the printer delivered the several thousand copies of the newsletter to the editor, she distributed copies around the personnel office. The phone started to ring almost immediately.

Others noticed what we hadn't. I had spelled the president's name "Olson" when he spells it "Olsen." Boy, did that create a stir. The editor ran around picking up every copy of the newsletter she could find and destroyed them. She had the printer make another print run, this time with the name spelled correctly. So beware—it's much easier to make those accuracy checks at the beginning of the writing process than after the fact when someone else reminds you.

The other check you'll want to make when you have the structure pretty well established is that you have followed the killer rules. Does your draft still meet your purpose? Have you written it to your audience? Have you met your audience's needs? Because writing is a process of discovery, you may have discovered new information or relationships between pieces of information that you must consider to make sure you've followed the killer rules.

What's next?

The next step after you have revised a draft is essentially the same as for a first draft. Let the revised draft cool. Although moves and changes made now seem right, they may not later, after several hours or days. Here again, find some other chores to do. Return some phone calls. Work on some other correspondence. Go to lunch or work out at the gym. Find an activity that will take your mind off the memo you've just been working on. In my case, I'm writing three memos, so I can move on to one of the others. I think I'll write the first draft of the memo to Purchasing.

Chapter 7

Getting Ready to Write to Purchasing

IMAGINE YOURSELF in the college book store picking up books for the new semester. You pick up a heavy and expensive Psychology text and thumb through it. As you scan the pages, you notice that each page is covered with words, from top to bottom, side to side, "wall-to-wall" as my colleagues sometimes put it. What's your reaction? A groan? Some comment about the author's parentage or that of the instructor who assigned the text?

Then, you walk to the shelf with the book for a graphic arts course you are taking. You thumb through this book and notice that there is a lot of white space, plenty of headings, and many illustrations. What is your reaction? Do you say to yourself, "I think I'll like this course"? Why? What does the look of a printed page have to do with your first impression of its contents? And what does any of this have to do with this book?

The visual aspects of business communication.

This book is about communicating in business, and the visual aspect of a piece of correspondence is significant to how it communicates. You'll note that in this book I've given you plenty of headings to keep you on track. You'll note in my examples that I've used headings and white space to keep the page attractive as well as to show structure.

An attractive page stands a better chance of being read than one which is jammed with words, thus providing the reader's eye with no visual resting place.

I've bought up this subject because the memo to purchasing provides a good opportunity to use good graphic presentation of information to advantage. I'll be providing part numbers and order rates, data that can cause confusion and errors if not presented in a "clean" way. If I make my reader search too hard for needed information, I shouldn't be surprised when that reader makes errors. The information may be available, but not accessible. Look over my shoulder now as I brainstorm and outline this memo to purchasing. But first, here is the doodling I did while brainstorming:

Purchasing memo

- should have info from other memos
- Audience is purchasing manager
  - buyer for capital equipment
  - buyer for supplies

- need dates to be in plant
- order rates / month

- Buyers need — machines & supplies
  - part #s
  - order rates
  - dates

- Give phone #s for questions
  - before cutover — me
  - after cutover — Steve Berg

Format to make info accessible so no mistakes

What is the purpose for this memo?

As I brainstormed, it became clear to me that this memo, like the one I wrote to production, has more than one purpose and more than one reader. It has to alert the purchasing manager to the fact that there will be a change in routine for his buyers. They will make some unscheduled capital equipment purchases, and they will order new glue supplies. Because the people who work for that manger will also be actively involved in the purchase of equipment and supplies, they will also need to be alerted. I came up with four purposes for this memo. Here are my notes as I worked toward those purposes:

Purpose
- To alert purchosing mgr about new staff
- give buyers all details
   - Part #s — machine - compony
   - Amounts — glue — base - compony
               solvent
   - dates
  - phone #s for question

Audience
- Purchosing manager
- Capital equipment buyer
- Supplies buyer

Needs
    use this list
    Format for easy reference

I added that last item because business writers don't always provide all of the details other departments need. For example, purchasing may need an account number or department code to fill out an order, and it is important that the person filling out the paperwork have a number to call to get the details straightened out quickly. Help your readers as much as possible, always.

Who is the audience for this memo?

The audience for this memo is pretty clear: the purchasing manager, a capital equipment buyer, and a supplies buyer. Unlike Bob Hollowell and Steve Berg, however, these people are strangers, and I will be writing, therefore, to a "position" rather than to a specific person. That is, I'll be writing to a generic purchasing manager who has credentials that I might assume all purchasing managers have. In this case a line manager (me) is asking a staff manager merely to perform a normal staff function. The purchasing staff members are technicians who buy capital equipment and supplies every day.

What does this audience need from the memo?

Because we are dealing with a professional staff doing its normal tasks, it is fairly easy for us to figure out the needs of this audience. The purchasing manager needs enough information to allocate resources and direct his or her staff to perform the functions requested by the time specified. The buyers, on the other hand, will need more detailed, specific information. Here's how I broke out these needs by specific audience.

Purchasing Manager—The purchasing manager needs general information about the capital equipment and supplies his staff has to buy. He'll need to know the dates the equipment and supplies are required and a contact person for questions he may have. He'll use this information to decide how many people to assign to this task.

Capital Equipment Buyer—For this scenario I'm assuming the new glue machines are expensive enough to be bought as capital equipment. The capital equipment buyer will need to know:

- Company from which to buy machines

- Model numbers of machines

- Numbers of each model to purchase

- Dates the machines must be in the plant

- Contact person(s) to answer questions about purchase

Supplies Buyer—The supplies buyer, like the capital equipment buyer, will need specific details about each of the supplies to be ordered. Those details are:

- Part numbers or names of each glue and solvent to be purchased

- The initial quantities to be ordered

- The rates at which these supplies should be reordered

- Contact person(s) to answer questions about this purchase

Although this memo seems fairly simple, I must be careful to give purchasing enough accurate information. If I give a wrong part number or reorder rate, I could be facing Bob Hollowell's wrath.

The outline for the memo to purchasing.

Here's what the outline for this memo looks like. Notice that it is shorter and contains fewer details than the memos to Hollowell and Berg because there is no need to pass on procedures or to provide background information. In this memo I'm only interested in giving the information necessary to place orders with external vendors.

Purpose

Glue machine purchase info

Glue purchasing info

Dates for initial shipment of machines and glues

Glue Machines

    2 Large machines

    1 Small machine

    Date needed

Glue

    3 types of glue

    Solvent for cleaning machines

    Date needed

    Reorder rates for each glue

Point of contact for additional information

    Your name (before cut over date)

    Steve Berg (after cut over date)

Some thoughts about this memo.

As with the memo I wrote to Steve Berg, I can expect this memo to be distributed widely. At the minimum, the purchasing manager will photocopy the memo and send copies to the purchasing supervisors for capital equipment and supplies. He will probably mark the appropriate part of the memo for each of them, asking them to take care of the details. The supervisors will copy the memo again, keeping a file copy and sending copies to the appropriate buyers. That's a fairly standard way to pass information in organizations. When you become part of an organization, learn how communication happens, so you can fit your messages into the "flow" for maximum effectiveness.

Here's the first draft of the memo to purchasing, marked up for structural revisions. Because we've already been through the chapter discussing how to make structural revisions, you should be able to figure out what I've done and why I've done it. The Appendix has my final memo to purchasing if you want to compare it to my initial marked-up draft.

Memo to Purchasing

Purpose

This memo contains order information for gluing machines, glue, and other supplies for the Model 1A Phaser Product Line. It includes the no-later-than dates for receiving the machines and initial shipments of glues.

Capital Equipment Requirements

intergalactic Industrial Equip. Corp.

You will need to order three gluing machines from ~~Acme Glue Products~~ Company, Inc. We have been working with them on our requirements, and they have supplied us with prototype machines for process testing. We need to have the following glue machines on hand no later than Thursday, October 30, 2213:

llE Q
~~Acme~~ Model GM-1701-L-03

llE Q
~~Acme~~ Model GM-1701-L-15

llE Q
~~Acme~~ Model GM-1701-S-11

These models have been specifically programmed for operations at stations 3, 11, and 15 on the Model 1A Phaser Product Line.

GLUE Q   *+ MONTHLY*
~~Production~~ Supplies Initial Requirements

The following glue supplies are necessary to start the new gluing process on the Model 1A Phaser Product Line no later than Thursday, October 30, 2213. You should order them from Acme Glue Products Company, Inc. There are three types of glue and one type of base mix, each with a different quantity:

Acme Part Number	Quantity
Acme GL-1701-03	14 Liters
Acme GL-1701-11	05 Liters
Acme GL-1701-15	22 Liters
Acme BM-1701-29	37 Liters
Acme Solvent #33	20 Liters

This is an initial order to start production and continue for one the first month. *[handwritten edits]*

Glue Supplies Reorder Rates

Please order the following quantities of glue, base mix, and solvent, to be delivered no later than the last day of each month. This order rate will remain in effect until you are notified to change it. The product line is scheduled to remain at this rate for at least three years.

[handwritten margin note: Combine with previous section]

Acme Part Number	Monthly Order Rate
Acme GL-1701-03	12 Liters
Acme GL-1701-11	04 Liters
Acme GL-1701-15	18 Liters
Acme BM-1701-29	30 Liters
Acme Solvent #33	15 Liters

[handwritten note: move to prev. ft]

Have all machines and supplies delivered to the Phaser Product Line in-plant warehouse and notify Henry Lancing at extension 5798 when they arrive.

[handwritten note: Put at end of previous section]

Contact for more information

Before November 1, 2213, contact <your name> at 5798

After November 1, 2213, contact Steve Berg at 5799

Chapter 8

Being Recognized as a Good Writer

As YOU WALK INTO your office after lunch, you go through the half dozen "while you were out" slips on your desk. The second one you look at notes that Bob Hollowell wants you to drop by his office. You can't help being a bit nervous as you call his secretary to make an appointment. Because it's Monday and Bob got your memo on Friday, you know what Bob wants to talk about.

When you return Hollowell's call, his secretary tells you to come down right away, as "Mr. Hollowell wants to see you as soon as possible." As you hurry down the hallway of executive offices, you wonder what you forgot or did wrong in the memo that Hollowell would want to talk about. It usually takes several days to get an appointment with him.

"Come on in," Hollowell shouts as you walk into the reception area in front of his office. He comes out to greet you, shakes your hand, and shows you to a leather covered chair in front of his desk.

"That was a really well written memo. Seems like you covered everything I had questions about."

Trying not to show your relief, you say, "Thanks, Bob, I tried to figure out what you wanted to know about the new process. Hope I had everything you needed."

"It has everything I'd expected and then some. The 'then some' is your suggestion to absorb the additional costs of the process rather than passing them on to Star Fleet. I showed the memo to Bill Cutler, and he jumped on your suggestion immediately."

Bill Cutler, you remember, is the Vice President for Customer Service, the person who hears from customers when things don't go according to plan, don't work right, are late, or have problems after being in service for some time.

"Bill said he felt we could really make some points with Star Fleet using your suggestion. He asked me to have you write a letter to Vice Admiral Van Gordon, the head of Star Fleet logistics, explaining the new gluing process and the fact that we will absorb the costs."

"Should I write it for his signature or yours?"

"His. He'd like to let them know he's looking out for Star Fleet interests here."

"When should I have it ready?"

"Bill will be out of the office until next Monday—going on a little vacation to the Bahamas. I'd say have it ready for him Monday."

"Should I run it past you first?"

"If you don't mind—because I can add my two cents if I feel the need. Bill will probably do some editing too. I've never seen anything come out of his office looking exactly like it went in. He has an undergraduate degree in English and a MBA from Wharton School, so he wants anything he signs to be perfect."

"I'll have a draft on your desk on Thursday morning to give you time to look at it and make any changes. Then I'll have Friday to get it ready for his signature."

"Sounds good. Do it like the memo you sent me, and you'll have no trouble. Bill said he wished he could get his staff write memos like yours."

As you grin your way out of the executive suites and head back for your office, you start thinking about the memo to Star Fleet. You wonder who Admiral Van Gordon is, and what will make Bill Cutler happy.

Planning the Letter to Admiral Van Gordon.

As usual, I'll show you what I would do to get this letter prepared and on Bill Cutler's desk. This time I have a slightly different task facing me because I'm writing a letter for someone else's signature and to someone I don't know. As a matter of fact, I've never heard of

Admiral Van Gordon. This letter goes outside of the corporation to one of its major customers. In this letter I'll not be concerned with the details of how to implement the new process, but with how the changes will be perceived by the person responsible for making sure the phasers issued to Star Fleet officers are serviceable and durable.

The lack of first hand knowledge about how Bill Cutler's letters sound and my ignorance about Admiral Van Gordon will require some research on my part—a task a young manager often faces. Managers and executives constantly ask their subordinates to write correspondence for their signatures, sometimes on subjects about which they're only generally informed. Letters of recommendation, for instance, responses to queries, or even details of major policy changes fall into this category.

A few months ago, for example, a client asked me if I'd write the letter her boss wanted sent to customers who were being surprised and angered by the increase in computer disk storage requirements for new software releases. Because I'd worked on a project that had also once irritated some customers, she figured I'd have a better idea than she would about what to say. I wrote the letter, passed it by her for approval, included her suggested changes, and put it into final form for her boss. After a few minor changes, he signed the letter, and customers today still get my letter advising them about the increase in computer disk storage requirements for future software releases.

This letter is a bit different, however, since the vice president who requested it isn't in my line of command and is not someone I'm familiar with. But then, as a newcomer on a staff you could get asked to write correspondence for your boss before you really get a chance to get solidly into your job. The older guys know how to be "too busy." At least that's the excuse they'll give you for pushing the writing off on you. I suspect the real reason is that few employees feel comfortable writing for the boss's signature.

What is my purpose in this letter to the Admiral?

Here I am again, using the same information and asking the same question—and again I expect a slightly different answer. The answers so far have included getting general information to a vice president, giving direction to subordinates, and providing purchasing information to a staff office. Now, as I think about the purpose of a letter to a customer, I need to think of Bill Cutler's purpose, rather than my purpose. What would Bill say if he were here and I could talk to him?

Don't ever rule out going to see the person you'll be writing for to ask questions to take some of the guesswork out of the planning. If the person who gives you the writing task will eventually sign the letter, ask as many questions as you can on the spot about purpose and audience. It's better to ask quesitons first than to guess at purpose and audience and have to start over from square one.

I remember once serving on a committee composed of Air Force colonels and very high ranking civilians. We had been meeting for several days on important programs to be included in the next Air Force budget. The chairman, a one-star general, made some summary comments, noted the kind of staff work he needed for our next meeting a week later, and asked if there were any questions. He glanced slowly up and down both sides of the long mahogany table, looking for either questions or quizzical faces, and seeing none, dismissed the committee.

The general got up, walked out of the room, and then the entire committee, as a group, besieged me with questions about what the general wanted. All I could say was that I didn't know the specifics of their particular area. I'm still baffled at why they didn't ask him when they had the chance. I guess no one wanted to be the first one to ask. Don't let vanity get in the way of asking the questions that you need answered when you're given any kind of assignment by your boss. Incidentally, I went to see the general, asked some of the questions the committee members should have asked, and relayed the answers to them.

Here are the handwritten notes I made while brainstorming for this letter:

Letter to Admiral V G.

- Customer - might be mad
- Letter for VP's signature
- Wants to know cause of problem

- wants to know fix for problem
- How much will it cost?
- Schedules
- make Kiow look good
  - quick fix
  - not caused by us
  - Not Costing S/F (good will)

Purpose
  - Explain problem + fix
  - Soothe any anger
  - build good will
  - give overview of schedule of fix

An additional "hidden" purpose for this letter is to build good will with Admiral Van Gordon, to show that Bull Cutler is looking out for Star Fleet's interests inside the corporation. The "good will" needs to be conveyed through the tone of the letter and by the inferences that Admiral Van Gordon can draw from the letter.

Who is the audience for this letter?

How would you handle this task? You've got to write to someone in an important position but about whom you have little information.

Do you guess? Not a good idea. Can you find out any of that information? Where? Since Bill Cutler asked me to write this letter, do you suppose he knows anything about the Admiral? Sure he does, but, he's on vacation in the Bahamas, isn't he? How about his secretary? You'd be surprised at how much the secretaries and administrative assistants in a corporation know about their boss's work. They make the phone calls, write up the memos of meetings, listen to their bosses complain, and generally come in contact with the people and information going through the office. Suppose I start by calling Bill Cutler's secretary.

Here's how my call to Bill's secretary, Helen Wells, went. First, she gave as much information as she knew about the Admiral and then put me on hold while she called the Admiral's administrative assistant. They often speak with each other as they arrange meetings, pass on information, and get their bosses together on the telephone. Helen came back on the line and gave me this information. Because I scribble badly making notes while on the phone, I've typed and edited them so you can read them.

- The admiral's full name is Mary E. Van Gordon.

- Has a MSEE degree from the Space Academy.

- Has 25 years of service in Star Fleet, the last 10 in logistics.

- Is very hard to deal with when things are going wrong.

- Gets very protective of Star Fleet when it appears that Star Fleet is in the wrong.

- Likes letters and memos to be short and to the point. Will not read any letter over two pages.

There's the audience. By the way, that last point describes the habits of many senior executives I've known both in government and in business. But what does all this information mean in terms of the letter?

Because Admiral Van Gordon has an MSEE and has been in logistics for the past 10 years, I can't expect her to be well versed in the molecular structure of glue, but I can expect her to know about the new teleporters. She is the head of Star Fleet logistics and will have been in on the decision to install the new teleporters. She'll probably know the principal working difference between the new and old teleporters. The implications of the new teleporters causing the problem will probably not be lost on her, and she might react negatively to that information, thinking we will blame Star Fleet for the phaser problems. She'll be ready to do battle to keep the cost of the solution down. I hope I can use her reaction to my advantage. After all, I'll be telling her that we won't charge Star Fleet for the repair of the unserviceable phasers or for the repair of phasers already in service.

What does Admiral Van Gordon need to know?

The Admiral will want to know what caused the problem and its solution. Having the problem already solved will help soften the implication that Star Fleet's new teleporters caused the problem, and the results of our testing should help her to feel better. Here are the notes I made as I brainstormed the Admiral's needs:

Admiral's needs

— To know cause of problem

— Fix for problem
— How to avoid in future

— How to fix phasers that break before
  they are replaced

— Cost of problem
  — Effect on program
  — How we will pay for it.

— Short letter

— we'll use glue in other space products

{ — what info to pass on to S/F Commanders
< as teleportation

Looking through these notes, I came up with this list of the Admiral's needs that I should consider as I write this letter.

- To understand how the cumulative effect of teleportation cause the problem so she can pass that information on to other staff agencies and space vehicles.

- To be assured the problem is fixed and won't reoccur.

- To pass the information on to Star Fleet commanders, so they can watch for the problem and take the appropriate action if older phasers start to come unglued.

- To know that the company will use the new glue in other space products that will be teleported.

- A letter shorter than two full pages. One page would be ideal, if possible.

Fortunately, most of the above information is already contained in the notes and memos I've written to Bob Hollowell and Steve Berg, so I won't have to dig for more. I can quickly outline and start writing.

Outlining the letter to Admiral Van Gordon.

I didn't do much brainstorming for this letter because I've already written three memos covering the same information. I looked back over my earlier notes and made a short list to serve as an outline. This list, like those for the other memos I've written, is rather cryptic, because the brainstorm session is merely a way of capturing information. I made these notes as I sat waiting for a dentist who said he'd "squeeze me in." Knowing that I would have some time to kill, I took my earlier notes, some paper, and a pencil along to capture my thoughts. You don't always have to be at your desk or in your work environment to do some brainstorming. I looked through my notes to see what information I'd need and where I'd find it. Here's that list:

Letter to Admiral VG (outline) ✓ when to find info

— Cause of problem — dr memo to Hallowell

— Solution to problem — memo to Hallowell

— Cost — mention — don't emphasize

— Fix of phones in service (new) break out in memo

— why Kiowa is paying (good will)
— Medical kits for example

Making an outline from lists and notes like this is an iterative process. First I brainstorm ideas and then consider what information I need and then where I find it. If I need more information, I would then decide where or how to get it. My brainstorming sessions always seems to go this way. I start with a list, break that list into its components, and then break those components into further divisions. Then when I run out of ideas, I look for some organizational pattern. I'll consider purpose, audience, and audience needs to get the process off to a running start. Making the outline, then, seems to come fairly easily, especially true when I already know most of the information for the memo or letter.

Here's the outline for the letter to Admiral Mary Van Gordon. Notice that it is more complete than the notes I've presented above. As in brainstorming, thinking about some items suggests others which in turn suggest others and other possible structures for the information.

The problem

    Glue joints failing after 25 teleportations

    New teleporters cause slight molecular change in glue

The solution

    New glue and procedures

    10,000 teleportations with no problems

    Tested 10 X more than S/F spec calls for

Fix for phasers in service

    150 failed phasers

    150 expected to fail

Schedule of fixes

    Ones in service that do not fail will be replaced when vessels are in space dock

    Ones that fail will be replaced immediately from the factory along with several spares in case or further failure

        Spares will count against replacement when in space dock

        Suggest old phasers on ship be replaced with spares before failure

Cost of fix

    Small relative to program for company

    Will not change cost of program to S/F

Reason for company absorbing cost of fix

    Good will

    Use of glue for other space products

        Medical kits

        Atmosphere sampling stations

        Future weapons and other products

Further questions to Bill Cutler, Vice President for Customer Service

Now I can write the letter to Admiral Van Gordon. The last in a series of pieces of correspondence, this one should be easier to write than the rest. I've thought most of the material through earlier and have already written about it. The most difficult part of this letter is the fact that I'm writing it for someone else's signature to someone, a large customer, whom I don't know.

Here's my draft:

Dear Admiral Van Gordon:

As you know, Model 1A Phasers have suddenly been failing in service. We asked our Testing Lab to look into the problem and come up with a fix for it. Here's a discussion of the problem, our solution to the problem, and the plan for implementing the ~~problem~~ _solution_.

Why our Phasers failed in service.

The Testing Lab noted immediately that the phasers in question had ~~under~~ _fewer than_ 25 teleportations logged and came from Star Fleet cruisers which used the new teleporters. These teleporters ~~degenerate~~ _decompose_ matter at the atomic level rather than at the molecular level as the older teleporters did. They suspected that the molecular structure of the glue in the phasers was somehow being changed, something no one expected. They ran some tests and found that there was a subtle but important change occuring in the glue after about 15 teleportations. Phasers that failed averaged about 25 teleportations, but one had failed with only 17 teleportations.

How we fixed the problem with the glue.

Working with the Acme Glue Products Company, Inc., our R & D Lab came up with a glue that has a slightly different molecular bonding than the glue we now use in production. We tested the glue in an atomic level teleporter, similar to your new teleporters, and found no change in the glue's molecular structure after 10,000 teleportations. We then took the phasers which had those 10,000 teleportations on them, and we tested them at ten times the normal testing we do to comply with your qualification specifications. Not one phaser failed. We're sure we have this problem fixed.

How we'll fix phasers now in service.

We'll ship the first 150 phasers to come off the production line with the new glue directly to Star Fleet cruisers to replace ones which have failed. Given the time necessary to get the new phasers to the fleet, we expect another 150 failures before we can replace all phasers now in service. We'll replace phasers which fail immediately from production stock. We'll replace them in space and provide several spares to count against final replacement numbers.

How we'll retrofit the rest of the fleet.

Our plan is to replace the phasers on each cruiser that now has phasers with the old glue as it comes into space dock to eliminate the need to replace phasers as they fail. We'll then replace the glue in those phasers and return them to service. We can do this and still maintain the delivery schedule we agreed to in our contract. That schedule has us delivering 10.000 phasers over the next three years. The replacement program will be small compared to the total program. so we will absorb that cost.

Why are we absorbing the cost?

The obvious reason for our absorbing the cost is to show that we are concerned about the quality of our products, even if a failure in a product is not a direct result of our materials, workmanship, or design. Another reason for this gesture of good will is that we will use this new glue in other products we manufacture for deep space, products like medical kits, atmospheric sampling stations, and other weapons which will undergo teleportation.

I hope this letter puts your mind at rest about the Model 1A Phaser problem and answers any questions you may have had. If you do have any other questions, please feel free to call me about them.

Sincerely,

Bill Cutler, Vice President
Customer Service
Kiowa Arms Manufacturing Corp., Inc.

It's now time to move on to revising the second drafts I've written. Once again, I'll ask you to drag up a chair and look over my shoulder as I work on all the memos and letters you've watched me write. I'll share a few techniques I've learned about fixing grammar, punctuation, and spelling, suggestions that are much less painful than some you've been exposed to. See you in the next chapter.

Chapter 9

Revising the Second Draft

AT THIS POINT in the writing process, I'm reasonably certain that I've got a good draft. On the first revision I concentrated on order, completeness, and eliminating excess information. I've made sure the structure is sound, so what's left is to check grammar, punctuation, readability, and spelling. First, I'll show you a method to help catch those grammar and punctuation problems that plague all writers. This method won't replace a good grounding in the rules or having a good style book like Strunk and White's *The Elements of Style,* but it will help you to spot potential problems.

Catching grammar and punctuation problems.

The secret of my method is to read your draft aloud. If it sounds good, it probably is good. If you have grammar or punctuation problems, reading your work aloud will help you hear the problems. Let me show you how. I'll give you two groups of words to read aloud. Read them slowly, as if you were reading from a book to a group of people. Pay attention to the intonation of your voice, particularly at the end of each of these two groups of words. Here they are:

the car ran a red light

it hit a truck in the intersection

What did your voice do? Did the tone drop at the end of each group? And did you pause? That's because each group is a sentence and should start with a capital and end with a period. I'll make a slight change in the words. Now, please read them aloud again.

when the car ran a red light

it hit a truck in the intersection

Do you hear the difference in the intonation of your voice? At the end of the first group, your voice stayed at a fairly constant level and you didn't pause as long. You instinctively realized that you don't need a period at the end of the first group but you do need a comma because the first group of words is now an introductory clause. Let's try one more reading. Again, read as if you were reading to a group.

The driver of the truck was injured the driver of the car was given a ticket.

How did that sentence sound? Did you have to read it two or three times to make sense out of it? When you figured out its meaning, did your voice drop after the word "injured," and did you pause? You did so because you realized instinctively that there are two sentences rather than one. Because you've been speaking English since you were a child, syntactical structures and their associated intonations and inflections are second nature to you.

What does this mean to you as a business writer? It means that for most cases in your writing, you can "hear" grammar and punctuation problems in your letters and memos, if you'll take the time to read them aloud. You don't *have* to read them so loudly that someone else could hear them, but doing so helps. If you whisper the words, that will be loud enough to "hear" grammar and punctuation problems. Remember when you were learning to read how the teacher told you not to move your lips because doing so slowed you down? Well, here you want to slow down to hear the words with your ear, your inner ear, so move your lips and form the words as you read them.

Making sure the draft is readable.

A side benefit of reading aloud is that you'll also find your tongue stumbling over the rough spots in your draft. If you have trouble smoothly saying something you've written, it needs work, because it doesn't have readability. What do I mean by readability? Well, readability is that quality of written language that makes it "sound" as if it were spoken rather than as if you were reading from a government document. When we speak, for instance, our sentences are of varying length. If they were all short sentences, we'd sound like those Dick and Jane readers we learned to read from. If all the sentences were long, we'd sound like a government directive or a textbook on a very dull subject.

A goal of business correspondence today is to sound as though the writer is speaking directly to the reader. I don't mean that you should put in all the "ahs" and false starts we have when we speak thoughtfully. I mean there should be a flow and vitality that our speech often has, but may not show in our prose. How do you get that quality into your writing? One technique is to imagine yourself standing face to face with your reader, speaking your memo or letter rather than dropping it into the mail. Would you be laughed at and laugh at yourself because of the pomposity? Would you sound like a petty bureaucrat from the government reading from the regulations?

Establish a warm, friendly, informal tone.

Here are a few hints to consider in your writing. Although they break with some of the rules you were given in English classes before, they describe the state of successful business communication. Today, successful business communicators want to establish a friendly, courteous tone in order to communicate information, because people respond more positively to a warm, friendly tone than they do to an officious, pompous one. Try these ideas in your writing.

Use personal pronouns: *I, you we, our, mine, your*
Use contractions: *can't, won't, haven't, isn't, I'll, you're*
Start an occasional sentences with a conjunction: *and, but, nor, for, or, yet*
Let some sentences end with a preposition: *with, on, to, in*
Ask questions—can you avoid answering when a writer uses a question?

I know some of you are rolling your eyes and thinking of the dire consequences if you "break these rules." Please stop before you decide to reject these ideas as being too informal for business writing. Would you accept the *Wall Street Journal* as a conservative newspaper that represents good usage in business writing? Find a copy, and turn to the editorial page. Pick any editorial on any day and see how many of the ideas I've just presented you'll find there. I read the *Journal* regularly and often see these style features. Even sentences that end with prepositions? Sure. Read the *Journal* and see how many you can come up with. That's the way business is conducted today, on a much more informal basis than in the past. Why? Because communicating through tone as well as with facts is the way the modern game is played.

A mid-course correction to this chapter.

I'd like to break this train of thought for just a minute to show you the revision process in action. I've been writing this chapter from a detailed outline, and I wrote the last paragraph about the *Journal* last night at about nine o'clock. I woke out of a sound sleep this morning thinking that I should give you examples from the editorial pages. But it is Saturday and the *Journal* isn't published today. So, I got up, went into the garage, reached into the trash can, and retrieved yesterday's *Journal*. I'm going to show you how secure I am in my claim that the *Journal* uses the stylistic devices I listed earlier. Here's part of the first paragraph on the page:

> George Bush ultimately will find a management team for the Department of Defense, but we hope he doesn't think he can stop there. . . . Let's hope he can find a DOD Secretary and Undersecretary who can help him with that.

Notice the use of personal pronouns and contractions. How much duller if the writer had used "the President" or "the newly elected President" instead of "he" and "him"? Five paragraphs later, the editorial discusses the problems a Pentagon general faces:

> But his freedom to offset the cuts with productivity gains has been restricted too. Under current rules, he can't pay overtime, even when it saves money. . . . Contracts must be "competed" even if it might mean losing a competent contractor and getting one who isn't.

Here a sentence starts with "But" and that startling conjunction is followed immediately with "his." Not by "the general," but by "his." What about the contractions "can't" and "isn't"? Do you see how they add to the readability of the editorial and make the words sound spoken? A real person, a live man or woman, speaks to us. The words aren't written dully by a bureaucratic cipher. Whether you agree or not with the ideas on that page, you have someone, not just a faceless newspaper, to agree or disagree with.

The opening line of the last paragraph of this editorial starts out asking a question:

> Is there anything the new Bush team can do about this, while of course conducting strategic planning and crisis management? Quite likely there is. But the President will have to commit his prestige to the effort, making a political issue out of congressional efforts to enlarge legitimate budgetary powers into direct DOD management.

How do you respond to a question like that? It really doesn't matter, except to notice that you do respond. Notice the punch of the short sentence following the question. It's an assertion that isn't weakened by putting a comma behind it and adding the next rather long sentence, just to avoid starting a sentence with "but." Starting that sentence with "But," with a capital "B," however, emphasizes the turn of thought into a different, more negative vein. That's effective business writing.

Before I pitch this smelly paper back into the garbage can, I'd like to quote from one more piece. It's an article, "Maybe Free Trade Is Good Politics," by Lindley H. Clark, Jr. I'll pick up the middle of a paragraph near the beginning of the article:

> So, by the time Congress and President Reagan agreed on a new trade bill this year, about the best that could be said about it was it could have been worse. Any president who wants to pursue protectionism now has, in the new legislation, all the power he could wish for.

What would your old high school English teacher say about starting that sentence with "So"? She'd let fly with the old red pen, wouldn't she? And how about ending that last sentence, the last one in the paragraph by the way—a place where it really sticks out—with the proposition "for"? Another shot of red ink. But that's today's style.

Even dunning letters from the IRS are friendly and warm. They don't scream at you as if you are a felon. They mention in a friendly way that perhaps you owe money, and you can either pay up or appeal through a channel they thoughtfully point out to you. Here are a few lines from a letter I got from the IRS two years ago:

> We may furnish this information to your state tax agency.

and later

> An amended tax return for 1985 is not necessary. However, it would be appropriate for you to review your prior and subsequent year tax returns

to determine if all income for those years was properly reported. If you find that it was not reported, you should promptly file an amended return (form 1040X) for each year and pay the additional tax and interest. Doing so now would be to your advantage since it will cost you less in interest and you may avoid certain penalties.

Now that's not written in the same clear style as the articles I've quoted from the *Journal,* but it isn't the old stuffy bureaucratic jargon the IRS used to be so famous for. It is readable and understandable. Although it's a dunning letter, it is friendly at the same time. The threat is clear but not heavy handed.

The IRS can even be nice when it owes you money. Here's part of a notice I got this year, a few months after I sent in my final tax payment:

We have corrected an error on your return for the above tax year. The correction is explained below. You may want to check your figures against ours. If you believe we made a mistake, please write to us and include the bottom part of this notice. You are entitled to the refund shown below unless you owe other taxes. If you have not yet received a check for this refund, it will be sent to you within 6 weeks from the date of this notice.

Again, although this isn't the most sparkling prose you've ever read, it is clear and relatively to the point. I might revise it to get rid of some passive voice and add a few contractions. But notice the short sentences and the logical flow. It's not exactly like a person speaking to you, but it comes close. It's a lot closer than "It has come to the attention of this office that a return has been filed in error by the above referenced taxpayer." By God, there may be some real flesh-and-blood people working in that office in Ogden, Utah.

Getting the final errors out.

Reading a draft aloud should help most punctuation and grammar errors in your correspondence and make it sound more like informal speech. You'll get better with time. If at first you feel a bit self-conscious, don't worry, because with practice, you'll hear those commas and periods in your sentences. Okay, let's assume you've read your paper aloud several times and have made it sound good. What's left to do? How about proofreading it for misspelled words and typos?

Although you will catch many of the misspelled words and typos as you check your paper for proper structure and read it aloud for readability, grammar, and punctuation, a few errors might sneak through. The longer the document, the more chance there is that something will slip past. So now, you need to make one more pass through the document, looking for nothing else but spelling errors. If you are using a word processing program with a spelling checker, by all means use it. But be careful. If you wrote "their" and you meant "there," the computer won't catch it. So how do you check your spelling if you don't have a spelling checker?

Go through your draft slowly, reading word by word. If you put a piece of paper or straight edge under the line you are checking, it will slow you down so you can look at each word more carefully. When you see a word you aren't one hundred percent sure of, put a check mark over the word. Go through the entire draft this way, and when you are through, get a dictionary and look up each word you've checked. Even if many of the words are correct as you've spelled them, don't feel that you are wasting time looking up words that are already spelled right. If you weren't sure of that spelling until you looked the word up, you may have saved yourself an embarrassing error. Remember my mistake with the company president's name?

One other trick some people use to check spelling is to start at the end of a draft and work back toward the front. That technique helps eliminate the tendency we all have of reading too quickly because we know what the next word is. The one drawback to this method of proofing, however, is that you probably won't catch the fact that you wanted "were" but spelled it "where." It may not be fair, but people will often judge the quality of your ideas by how well you spell. They will wonder how careful you are with ideas if you aren't careful with spelling. Don't let anyone question your ideas because of something as simple and mechanical as getting the words spelled right.

On the same subject, here's one set of words that gives me and a lot of people fits. The two almost identical words are "its" and "it's." You could try to remember that "its" is a possessive pronoun while "it's" is a contraction. But when you write "the computer's maintenance costs" using an apostrophe to show possession, you may later write "it's original cost," again using the apostrophe to show possession. How can you avoid this error? I've trained myself to stop reading every time I see either "its" or "it's." I consciously replace either word I see with "it is." If "it is" fits, then I write "it's." If "it is" doesn't fit, then I write "its." That works for me. You can use my method until you find one that works for you. Careful readers will catch this mistake because it's one of the most common. So, beware!

The final step in getting rid of the last five percent of your errors is to have someone else read your draft. You may have missed a comma or grammatical point earlier. You may have overlooked a typo or misspelled word. You may have left some point unclear. Another reader's eyes and ears are invaluable here, especially if they belong to someone who meets your audience's qualifications. If that reader is one of the group of people the letter or memo is going to, then a point your proofreader doesn't understand may not be clear to the rest of your audience either. Remember, it is your responsibility to be clear. It is not your reader's responsibility to figure out what you meant. I have my students swap papers and check each other's for these errors. I'd rather have my students see a fellow student find and correct them and see the advantage of having another set of eyes read the paper than for me to have to mark those errors as Miss Grundy did.

Reading my draft memo to Hollowell aloud.

I've revised the drafts of all three memos and the letter to Admiral Van Gordon. Pull up a chair and follow me through each of these second drafts to see the kind of revisions I made to get them ready to send off. I used the principles I've discussed in this chapter, starting by reading them aloud. I'll provide examples of sentences and paragraphs from each memo and letter to show you the changes I've made and tell you why I made them. Although I discussed grammar, punctuation, and readability separately earlier in the chapter, when you read your work aloud, you'll catch these problems as they come along. So I'll show you all the changes I made and discuss my reasons for making them.

Let's start with the memo I wrote for Bob Hollowell, the Vice President for Manufacturing. Here's what the marked-up draft looks like:

Background

Starfleet ~~ran into~~ *started having* problems with our Model 1A Phaser when they ~~modified~~ *installed new*

~~the~~ teleporters on ~~some of the~~ *new* ~~newer~~ fleet cruisers. The old teleporters

~~reduced~~ *decomposed* matter to the molecular level while the new teleporters ~~reduce~~ *decompose it*

matter to the atomic level. Apparently, reducing matter to the atomic level
causes matter to be improperly reassembled [in areas with strong magnetic
fields] This new matter reduction, however, has caused problems with the
glue we use in the Model 1A Phaser.   *This new method of teleporting matter.*

We have been using the same glue in the Model 1A Phaser for the past
three years with no problems. Starfleet has phasers which have gone
through over 1000 teleportations with no reduction in tensile or shear
strength of the glue. With the new atomic level teleporters, however, the
glue in the phasers has failed after less than 25 teleportations. This is
obviously not a satisfactory performance for either Starfleet or us.

The materials lab has worked for three months to come up with a new glue
to fix the problem. Testing done on the glue after 10,000 teleportations and
to 10 times the normal testing to Starfleet specs has produced no failures .

Production Changes

Fortunately, there are few changes necessary to use the new glue or gluing
procedure. Three new gluing machines will replace older ones at the same
stations on the line and the assembly procedures are very similar to the ones
now in use. There is a slight difference in the curing process for the new
glue having to do with temperature and time, not equipment or process.
We'll conduct a short training class on October 15, 2213, to acquaint the

will train

assemblers ~~with~~ the new procedures. The production supervisors ~~will learn~~ in the new processes from [the lab people who developed the glue] and the supervisors will conduct the classes.
^ production

stet

I'll write a memo ~~with appropriate attachments~~ to Steve Berg, the production
to provide
line manager, ~~covering~~ details of training schedules, installation and
operation
production procedures and machine ~~maintenance~~

Instructions for Purchasing

also
I'm preparing a memo for purchasing to alert them ~~for the need~~ to buy the
three new gluing machines from Interglactic Industrial Equipment
the
Corporation and to order a new ~~type of~~ glue from Acme Glue Products
Company, Inc. I'll include ~~spare parts for the machines and~~ order rates for
^ monthly
the glue in that memo.

Financial Effects of New Gluing Process

I've used
current
~~Using~~ the plan to build 10 K phasers over the next three years ~~to complete~~
to construct
~~the Model 1A Phaser contract~~ with Starfleet ~~as a base~~, here are the unit cost
^ for
increases:

- New gluing machines add $0.92

- Improved glue adds   0.01

- Labor costs   0.00

We have already delivered 3.7 K phasers to Starfleet and will have to call
them back to reglue them with the improved glue. One hundred and fifty

phasers have ~~already~~ *[q]* failed in service. I expect another 150 to fail before we can replace them with new phasers. Here are the unit costs to repair the phasers already in service:

- 150 failed phasers $50.37

- 150 phasers likely to fail   50.37

- 3.4 K repaired at factory   20.25

We expect to repair the 3.4 K phasers at a rate of 1700 per month, which should get ~~them all~~ *[all phasers]* repaired and back in service in two months, ~~once~~ *[after]* we start the repair cycle. We'll need to work ~~out~~ the details of this cycle with Starfleet. For the time being, we can increase our production rate slightly and use the excess to replace failed units from the field.

The ~~total increased~~ *[added]* cost of the new gluing process for the Model 1A Phaser product line is:

- Cost of new machines $9,200.00

- Added cost of glue   100.00

- Repair existing units   15,111.00   *[or]*

Total ~~Increased~~ *[added]* Cost $24,411.00

Total per unit Cost $2.44

This will reduce the profit per unit from $53.74 to $51.30. I've not included the R & D costs in the figures because we can spread those across all our deep space product lines making the delta cost minimal.

As you can see, installing the new machines and using the new glue will
have a relatively small effect on our profit forecasts for the Model 1 A Phaser
product line. Because of this small effect, I've included a recommendation ~~as~~ *about*
~~to~~ how ~~we may want~~ to handle the charges to Starfleet.

Recommendations

The glue we have been using in the Model 1 A Phasers meets all Starfleet
specs, and none have failed in service except with the new teleporters. We
could charge ~~the~~ *our* additional costs ~~we'll bear~~ to Starfleet and be within our
legal rights. Our phasers, however, are failing in service and that's not good
for our reputation for quality. The delta cost to fix the problem doesn't cut
into our profit margin very much, and the glue we've developed gives us a
competitive advantage we can exploit immediately *in* ~~on~~ other deep space
products.

My recommendation is that we tell Starfleet about the new glue, give them
the data on the testing we've done, and tell them we'll absorb the additional
cost of manufacture and retrofit of phasers already in service.

put purpose of section right up front

If you have any questions on the data or procedures I've outlined in this
memo, please don't hesitate to call me at extension 5798.

Look at the beginning of the first paragraph. You can see that I've
made wholesale changes. The first sentence didn't "sound" smooth as
I read it. The words "ran into" sounded a bit too much like an
accident, so I replaced them with "started having." To my ear, that
sounded more like the situation. Then I realized that the problems
didn't start when Star Fleet "modified the teleporters," but rather
when they installed them on the new fleet cruisers. So I rewrote that
sentence to be more accurate. Because the final two sentences in the

paragraph seemed to ramble, I did some major surgery on them. The phrase "in areas with strong magnetic fields" seemed out of place, and the phrase "This new matter reduction" seemed both redundant and inaccurate. I had some problems with those two sentences, as the marked up copy shows. Here's the way the rewritten paragraph came out:

> Star Fleet started having problems with our Model 1A Phaser when they installed new teleporters on new fleet cruisers. The old teleporters decompose matter to the molecular level while the new teleporters decompose it to the atomic level. Apparently, reducing matter to the atomic level in areas with strong magnetic fields sometimes causes matter to be improperly reassembled and has caused the problems with the glue in the Model 1A Phaser.

An example of the usefulness of reading your writing aloud just happened as I reread this passage. I pulled up the latest copy of the draft I was revising on my computer, copied the paragraph electronically, and pasted it into this chapter. When I read it aloud again to see how my revisions had helped, I stumbled over the phrase "when they new teleporters" and realized that I had left out "installed." I made the correction in the passage quoted above and on the file containing the revised memo. Wouldn't want to make a mistake like that in a memo to Hollowell.

Three paragraphs later I discuss "Production Changes," and the paragraph seemed to need help when I read it aloud. There seemed to be a need for clarity, brevity, and simplicity in this paragraph. Look back at the marked-up draft to see what the original looked like. Here's the revised paragraph:

Production Changes

Fortunately, we'll have only a few changes to make to use the new glues. Three new gluing machines will replace older ones at the same stations on the line. The assembly procedures are very similar to the ones now in use. There is a slight difference in the curing process for the new glue. The new process involves changes in temperature and time, not equipment or process. We'll conduct a short training class on October 15, 2213, to show the assemblers the new procedures. The lab people who developed the glue will train the production supervisors in the new processes. The supervisors will conduct the production classes.

As I reread this paragraph, I think I may revise it again because several important items seem to be buried. The sentences don't read well because they are choppy, but I don't want to bury important information by running several sentences together. What would they look like if I made a list out of the important points? Let's do that and see. Here's one of the advantages of electronic writing.

Production Changes

Fortunately, we'll have only a few changes to make to use the new glues:

- Three new gluing machines will replace older ones at the same stations on the line.
- The assembly procedures are very similar to the ones now in use.
- There is a slight difference in the curing process for the new glue.

The new curing process involves changes in temperature and time, not equipment or process. We'll conduct a short training class on October 15, 2213, to show the assemblers the new procedures. The lab people who developed the glue will train the production supervisors in the new processes. The supervisors will conduct the production classes.

I like this version much better. The whole process, pulling up the original paragraph, copying it and pasting it in, revising it, and pasting the revised paragraph back into the original file, took under five minutes. Although using a computer or word processor doesn't help your basic writing skills, it does let you use those skills more efficiently. What are the chances that I would have made that change if I had to type the memo over again?

At the end of this memo I discovered that I needed to do a bit more restructuring. I hadn't noticed during the first revision that I put my recommendations at the end of the section called "Recommendations." Because the recommendation sets the context for the rationale, I believe you should state your message at the beginning of a memo, letter, or section and provide the rationale afterward. So, I revised this section. Look back at the marked-up draft and check it with the revised version.

Recommendations

My recommendation is that we tell Star Fleet about the new glue, give them the data on the testing we've done, and tell them we'll absorb the additional cost of manufacture and retrofit of phasers already in service.

The glue we have been using in the Model 1A Phasers meets all Star Fleet specs, and none have failed in service except with the new teleporters. We could charge our additional costs to Star Fleet and be within our legal rights. Our phasers, however, are failing in service and that hurts our reputation for quality. The delta cost to fix the problem doesn't cut into our profit margin very much, and the glue we've developed gives us a competitive advantage we can exploit immediately in other deep space products.

This revision seems to have more force, as it should. After all, I'm suggesting that Kiowa not charge a customer for something that is the customer's fault. In the unrevised version I seemed to sneak up to the recommendation as if not really convinced that it is the right thing to do. I like the revision better.

I included this revision here because I wanted to show that structural problems can show up at any time during the revision process, not just on that first pass. On the other hand, I fixed the spelling, grammar, punctuation, and readability problems I noticed during the first revision, but I didn't spend time looking for them. I took care of those I noticed.

Reading my draft memo to Berg aloud.

Here are some of the changes I made during this second revision pass in the memo to Steve Berg and his production people. Most of the revision in this memo came at the front of the memo where the discussion is more general. The sections containing the new procedures were fairly simple to start with and needed little revision on this pass. Here's a paragraph about "New Gluing Procedures" that needs extensive revision:

New Gluing Procedures

The gluing procedures contained in this memo are based on all of the assemblers who work at stations 3, 11, and 15 undergoing training on them on October 15, 2213. These procedures will go into effect on the November 3, 2213. Because the procedures are so similar to the current ones, the number of assemblers is exactly the same. The checklists attached at the end of this memo contain the procedures for each station, and the curing process all stations will use are at the end of the station procedures. These procedures replace the ones now in the process books for each station.

And here is the revised version:

New Gluing Procedures

The gluing procedures contained in this memo assume that assemblers who work at stations 3, 11, and 15 will be trained on October 15, 2213. We'll start using these procedures on November 3, 2213. Because the procedures are so similar to the current ones, the number of assemblers is exactly the same. The checklists attached at the end of the memo contain the procedures for each station. The curing process for all three stations is at the end of the gluing procedures and replaces the one now in the process books for each station.

This paragraph is more forceful because I've eliminated a lot of phrases that sound rather bureaucratic. For example, in the first sentence the words "are based on all of the" are replaced by "assume that." And in the next sentence the words "These procedures will go into effect" become "We'll start using these procedures." The revision is more to the point and includes me as part of the team. After all, Steve does work for me.

Never forget that unclear or unforceful writing can cause grief in any instructional memo. Here is an example from the memo to production where I'm telling the installation crew about the orientation of a mounting bracket relative to the operator's position:

Installing the mounting bracket:

1.   Locate the center of the current mounting bracket and use that as the center of the new mounting bracket. The new bracket is several inches larger than the old one. The open side of the new bracket should face the operator's position, which is directly in front of the machine.

And here is the rewritten passage.

Installing the mounting bracket:

1. Locate the center of the current mounting bracket and use it as the center of the new mounting bracket. The new bracket is several inches larger than the old one. Make sure the open side of the new bracket faces the operator's position, directly in front of the machine.

Notice how with only minor changes the instructions are much clearer. The person reading them is responsible to "Make sure." With the original passage, the bracket somehow "should face." No one was responsible to see that the orientation was right. That kind of oversight in communication is what often causes failures in processes, procedures, and business. Taking the time to read your memos and letters aloud can help you eliminate this kind of unclear prose.

Reading my memo to purchasing aloud.

I discovered a similar lack of clarity in my memo to the purchasing group. I've included the entire memo here so you can see the changes I made. Probably because this information is pretty straight forward and I've been through it several times, I didn't need to make any changes. I'm not trying to explain a process or the reasons for change, only to provide part numbers, order rates, and dates.

Memo to Purchasing

Purpose

This memo contains order information for gluing machines, glue, and other supplies for the Model 1A Phaser Product Line. It includes the no-later-than dates for receiving the machines and initial shipments of glues.

Capital Equipment Requirements

You will need to order three gluing machines from Interglactic Industrial Equipment Corp. (IIEC) We have been working with them on our requirements, and they have supplied us with prototype machines for process testing We need to have the following glue machines on hand no later than Thursday, October 30, 2213:

        IIEC Model GM-1701-L-03

        IIEC Model GM-1701-L-15

        IIEC Model GM-1701-S-11

These models have been specifically programmed for operations at stations 3, 11, and 15 on the Model 1A Phaser Product Line.

Production Supplies Inital Requirements

Please order the following glue supplies from Acme Glue Products Company, Inc., to start the new gluing process on the Model 1A Phaser Product Line. We'll need the initial order no later than Thursday, October 23, 2213. The first delivery at the monthly reorder rates should be no later than November 30, 2213, and monthly deliveries should be on hand no later than the last day of each month thereafter.

Acme Part Number	Initial Quantity	Monthly Reorder Rate
Acme GL 1701 03	14 Liters	12 Liters
Acme GL-1701-11	05 Liters	04 Liters
Acme GL 1701 15	22 Liters	18 Liters
Acme BM-1701-29	37 Liters	30 Liters
Acme Solvent #33	20 Liters	15 Liters

Please have all machines and initial supplies delivered to the Phaser Product Line in-plant warehouse and notify Henry Lancing at extension 5798 when they arrive. And handle monthly supply orders in the usual way.

Contact for more information

Before November 1, 2213, contact ‹Your Name› at 5798

After November 1, 2213, contact Steve Berg at 5799

Here are the reasons for some of the changes I made. In the paragraph "Capital Equipment Requirements," I had a sentence that read:

We need to have the following glue machines on hand no later than Thursday, October 30, 2213:

This clause is followed by a listing of three types of machines that purchasing is to order from the Interglactic Industrial Equipment Corp. But I sensed something missing as I read this paragraph aloud. Something just didn't sound right. On about the third reading I realized I had forgotten to tell purchasing how many of each machine to order. The rewritten sentence says:

We need to have one of each of the following glue machines on hand no later than Thursday, October 30, 2213:

The previous wording would have resulted in a phone call from purchasing to find out the number of machines to order, thus slowing the order process and perhaps delaying the implementation of the new glue procedures. How would Bob Hollowell respond to that? I'm sure I don't want to know first hand.

The next paragraph in the memo, one titled "Production Supplies Initial Requirements," needed some help to make it clearer and more readable. Look back at the memo for the original paragraph and compare it to the revised one.

Production Supplies Requirements

Please order these glue supplies from Acme Glue Products Company, Inc., for the new gluing process on the Model 1A Phaser Product Line. We'll need the initial order no later than Thursday, October 23, 2213. The first delivery at the monthly reorder rates should be no later than November 30, 2213, and each monthly delivery no later than the last day of the month.

First notice that I had to reword the title of this section to make it more accurate. When I revised for structure, I missed the word "initial" in the title. I rewrote the last sentence to make wording about the "first delivery" and "each monthly delivery" to eliminate wordiness and redundancy. For example the phrase "should be on hand" is already implied by the first part of the sentence and the context.

Reading my letter to Admiral Van Gordon aloud

Finally, let's look at the revisions I made to the letter to Admiral Mary Van Gordon as a result of reading it aloud. You'll remember that she likes short, well-written correspondence. I don't want to make mistakes here because then I'd have two vice presidents after me. Here's a copy of the entire letter with my revision marks:

Dear Admiral Van Gordon:

As you know, Model 1A Phasers have suddenly been failing in service. We
~~had a~~ ~~asked~~ our Testing Lab ~~to~~ look into the problem and come up with a ~~fix for it~~ solution.
Here's a discussion of the problem, our solution to the problem, and the plan
for implementing the ~~problem~~ solution.

Why our Phasers failed in service.

The Testing Lab noted immediately that the phasers in question had ~~been through~~ fewer
than 25 teleportations ~~logged~~ and came from Star Fleet cruisers which used
the new teleporters. These teleporters decompose matter ~~at~~ to the atomic level
rather than ~~at~~ to the molecular level as the older teleporters did. The ~~lab engineers~~
suspected that the molecular structure of the glue in the phasers was
somehow being changed, something no one expected. They ran some tests
and found that there was a subtle but important change occurring in the glue
after about 15 teleportations. Phasers that failed averaged about 20
teleportations, but one had failed with only 17 ~~teleportations~~.

How we fixed the problem with the glue.

Working with the Acme Glue Products Company, Inc., our R & D Lab came up
with a glue that has a slightly ~~different~~ stronger molecular bonding than the glue we
now use ~~in production~~. We tested the glue in an atomic level teleporter,
similar to your new teleporters, and found no change in the glue's molecular
structure after 10,000 teleportations. We then took the phasers which had
~~been through~~ ~~those~~ 10,000 teleportations ~~on them~~ and we tested them at ten times ~~the~~
~~normal testing we do to comply with~~ ~~more than~~ your qualification specifications. Not
one phaser failed. We're sure we have this problem fixed.

How we'll fix phasers now in service.

We *will* ship the first 150 phasers to come off the production line with the new
glue directly to Star Fleet cruisers to replace ones which have failed. Given
[our production ramp up with the new glue] *time to get phasers to the fleet* we expect another 150 failures
before we can replace all phasers now in service. We'll replace phasers
which fail immediately from production stock. We'll replace them in space
and provide several spares to count against final replacement numbers.

How we'll retrofit the rest of the fleet.

Our plan is to replace the phasers on each cruiser that now has phasers with
the old glue as it comes into space dock to eliminate the need to replace
phasers as they fail. We'll then replace the glue in those phasers and return
them to service. We can do this and still maintain the delivery schedule we
agreed to in our contract. That schedule has us delivering 10,000 phasers
over the next three years. The replacement program will be small compared
to the total program, so we will absorb that cost.

Why are we absorbing the cost?

The obvious reason for our absorbing the cost is to show that we are
concerned about the quality of our products, even if a failure in a product is
not a direct result of our materials, workmanship, or design. Another reason
for this gesture of good will is that we will use this new glue in other
products we manufacture for deep space, products like medical kits,
atmospheric sampling stations, and other weapons which will undergo
teleportation.

I hope this letter puts your mind at rest about the Model 1A Phaser problem and answers any questions you may have had. If you do have any other questions, please feel free to call me about them.

Sincerely,

Bill Cutler, Vice President

Customer Service

Kiowa Arms Manufacturing Corp., Inc.

The paragraph dealing with "How we fixed the problem with the glue" needed a bit of help. Look at the original and compare it with this revised version.

How we fixed the problem with the glue.

Working with the Acme Glue Products Company, Inc., our R & D Lab came up with a glue that has a slightly stronger molecular bonding than the glue we now use. We tested the glue in an atomic level teleporter, similar to your new teleporters, and found no change in the glue's molecular structure after 10,000 teleportations. We then took the phasers which had been through 10,000 teleportations and tested them at ten times Star Fleet qualification specifications. Not one phaser failed. We're sure we have this problem fixed.

The fact that the molecular bonding in the new glue is "different" is of no interest to Admiral Van Gordon, nor does it make my point to her. That the molecular bonding is "stronger" is important, hence the change. The sentence starting "We then took . . ." is long enough that I ran out of breath reading it, a definite clue to a problem. The reason it was too long is that there were many unnecessary words in it. Getting rid of "the normal testing we do to comply with" helps. The shorter sentence is to the point and more easily understood.

I've got one final paragraph to look at. I've described the problem and the solution to Admiral Van Gordon; now I want to tell her "How we'll retrofit the rest of the fleet." Look back to the memo if you want to see the original paragraph. Check it against the revised one here.

How we'll retrofit the rest of the fleet.

Our plan is to replace the phasers on each cruiser as it comes into space dock for periodic maintenance and refitting. We'll then replace the glue in those phasers and return them to service. We can do this and still maintain the delivery schedule we agreed to in our contract. That schedule has us delivering 10,000 phasers over the next three years. The replacement program will be small compared to the total program, so we will absorb that cost.

All the phasers now in service have the old glue, so what else would we replace? So I cut the phrase "that now has phasers with the old glue," and ". . . eliminate the need to replace phasers as they fail." It would be rather stupid, unsafe, and uneconomical to replace phasers only as they fail. The paragraph is shorter and much clearer in the new version.

What's next?

Next, I have to get my drafts into final shape. But first, let's review the revising process I've used. You've seen the readability revisions I made in my drafts after first revising them for structural problems. The important points are that reading aloud will help you "hear" problems you don't "see" and will help you catch structural problems you missed the first time through the draft. I've broken the revision process into sequential steps, but focusing on the primary step doesn't imply that you can't fix other problems when you see or hear them. Because your focus is different in each step of the process, you will often catch other unrelated problems. It's similar to remembering that person's name you couldn't think of earlier in the day when you are doing something else and no longer trying so hard to think of it. Your subconscious works on the problem while you are doing something else. Just so, your subconscious can spot or hear other problems in your draft while you are looking for unrelated ones. Each step in the process helps the other ones, and they all help you communicate better.

Chapter 10

Producing Final Copies

You've watched me write and revise a final draft, and now it's time to get the final copy ready. The final copies of the three memos and the one letter I've been writing are in the appendix for you to read. In this chapter, though, I'd like to discuss some ways to get business correspondence into final form, that is, ready for you put into the mail.

Producing the final copy on a typewriter.

After you've gone through two major revisions as I've done, you are ready to send your memo or letter. But as you get your draft ready to type in final form, it's a good idea to read through it one last time, especially if you've let the final draft cool a bit again. Put the final draft with its editing marks on the desk in front of you and read it aloud. You'd be surprised at how often the exact wording you've been looking for, but couldn't come up with earlier, suggests itself to you because your subconscious has been working while you were doing other tasks.

Even if you have to type the document again, don't be afraid to try new wording. Make sure by reading the whole paragraph again that the new wording fits smoothly into the rest of the paragraph. If the rewording is extensive—you've rewritten most of a paragraph—you might want to read the paragraphs before and after to make sure the flow of ideas isn't disturbed by the new wording.

Changes are much easier with a computer.

The computer makes this kind of change very easy. Pull the file up on the screen, and when you find a sentence you want to revise, try this procedure. Leave the old sentence on the screen, hit the return key a couple of times to make room for a new sentence, and type it in. Now you can see both versions and choose between them. You may find that neither is exactly what you want, so pick parts of both to make a third version you like best. Putting this one on the screen with the other two gives you a chance to see all three before deciding. Then, you can delete the sentences you don't want and move on to the next paragraph. Oh, the joy of writing on a computer!

Printing from your computer.

When you print your final copy from a computer, you often have a choice of printers. Each type of printer uses a different process for getting words on the paper and usually has a different look. For example, both the daisy wheel printer and the laser printer produce "letter quality" documents. Letter quality means that the type looks as though it was typed on an electric typewriter by an 80 words-per-minute typist who never makes mistakes.

Some businesses, however, use dot matrix printers which produce documents that are not as clean and crisp looking as those from daisy wheel or laser printers. You can make your documents look good on a dot matrix printer if you use a new or almost new ribbon for your final copy. Because the ribbons in most dot matrix printers cycle back and forth from end to end, they get less dark with each pass through the print head. At times I've resorted to replacing the ribbon in the printer for my final copy, and then putting the old one back for draft documents. If you are concerned about the cost of ribbons, this method is one way to keep that expense down.

Getting paper through the computer printer.

You'll often print business correspondence, including internal memos, on company letterhead or on memo forms. That's no problem when you're using a typewriter, but can cause problems when you write on a computer. With some printers, you will have to feed letterhead into the printer by hand, sheet by sheet. Although hand feeding a letter or two is no big deal, hand feeding several hundred letters can be time consuming. Many printers, including daisy wheel and dot matrix printers, have optional "sheet feeder" attachments which automatically feed paper to the printer one sheet at a time. You can put a sheaf of company letterhead into the sheet feeder and let it print your letters on them. Every laser printer I've seen uses a sheet feeder to feed the paper to the print mechanism. Here again, just load the paper tray, much like the ones on photocopy machines, with letterhead or memo forms, and you're on your way.

Another way to get paper through your printer without having to feed it by hand is to use the printer's tractor feed mechanism and continuous form paper. Continuous form paper comes in one long, continuous strip, perforated between sheets so it tears apart easily. It is recognizable by the perforated strips on both sides of the page. These strips have holes that engage teeth in the tractor feed mechanism, which pulls the paper through the printer in one continuous stream until the printing job is finished. Paper companies can provide company letterhead or memo blanks on continuous form paper.

Although continuous form paper is very handy, it has one drawback. Because you must tear the sheets apart and tear the perforated tractor strips from the sides, the paper has rough edges at the perforations. These rough edges mean that your document doesn't look quite as slick as one from a sheet fed machine. You'll have to decide between the convenience and speed of tractor-fed paper and the quality look of sheet-fed paper. Or compromise and use tractor-fed paper for internal memos and letters, and sheet-fed paper for letters to important customers. While that's a business decision, considering your Purpose, Audience, and Audience Needs might help you make that decision.

Merge programs for personalized letters.

Most word processing programs have a merge feature that lets you type one master letter containing special codes to mark places where you want to print information that is specific to each recipient. You also create a data file containing the unique information for each recipient. A data file might contain information such as the person's name, address, company name, first name or nickname, account number, and other facts pertaining only to that person. When you print the master letter, the program "merges" the master and data files and prints a letter for each entry in your data file. If you have fifty entries in your data file, the program will print a personalized letter for each person or company in that file.

Here's a data file I use to send letters to the President and Vice President of the United States, my congressional delegation, and other federal officials when I have something to gripe about or praise them about.

Name, Address, City, State, Zip, Name1

President George Bush, 1600 Pennsylvania Ave NW, Washington DC, 20500, President Bush

Vice President Dan Quayle, 1600 Pennsylvania Ave NW, Washington DC, 20500, Vice President Quayle

Senator William L. Armstrong, 528 Hart Office Building, Washington DC, 20510, Senator Armstrong

Senator Timothy E. Wirth, 237 Russell Office Building, Washington DC, 20510, Senator Wirth

Congressman Joel Hefley, 508 Cannon HOB, Washington DC, 20515, Mr. Hefley

Congresswoman Pat Schroeder, House of Representatives, Washington DC, 20515, Ms. Schroeder

Secretary of Defense Dick Cheney, DOD Pentagon, Washington DC, 20301-1155, Mr. Secretary

General Colin Powell, JCS Pentagon, Washington DC, 20301-115, General Powell

Notice that the first entry contains terms which explain each item between the commas. The master letter uses these terms to call for the unique data in each entry. For example, where I want the person's name to appear in the letter, I type «Name» and the each person's name will appear there. If I want to use a form of address like "President Bush," I put the term «Name1» in that place.

Because this letter was about a Department of Defense matter, I included the Secretary of Defense and Chairman of the Joint Chiefs of Staff. If I were writing about National Parks, I'd remove the DOD officials and add some Department of the Interior and Department of Agriculture names.

This feature allows you to send personalized letters to many people at once. If you retain the data file and make minor changes as I mentioned I do in my federal file, you can write master letters when you need to communicate with the people in that data file. They'll get a personalized letter each time. For example, you might have a data file for every sales person in a district, one for every manager in the district, one for every large customer, and one for every small customer. You can write four master letters and print letters for every person on these four lists in a short time.

The image created by this kind of "form" letter is much better than one created by a form letter that has been duplicated on a photocopy machine and has had the blanks filled in on a typewriter. Everyone knows this is a form letter—it looks and reads like a form letter. Your audience might suspect that your merged letter is a form letter because of its contents, but its neatness and personal nature make people ignore that possibility.

Reach out and communicate with electronic mail.

I discussed electronic mail in an earlier chapter, but I want to mention it again here. The earlier discussion centered on formatting mail to take advantage of the computer screen and avoid its restrictions. Electronic mail has several attributes. First, your message gets to many people instantly. Because most electronic mail programs have a feature that lets you send a message to a list of people all at once, you can create lists of people you communicate with frequently. Each list can be specialized for topics, position in the organization, or function. You write your message, specify which list to use, and press the return key to send the message instantly to everyone on the list.

A second attribute of electronic mail is its immediacy—perhaps the most significant reason for using it. For some reason, mail on a computer screen seems to require immediate reading and response. Maybe it's that little cursor blinking, seeming to await some reaction and action. If you want to convey urgency, use electronic mail. If you want to convey the image of class, use paper—for formal announcements and invitations. For those times when you need to get or send information now, to conclude negotiations with a client, to complete a report, to get information quickly to the field, electronic mail is perfect. The Fax machine is another electronic tool that lets you move information quickly. And these machines are showing up in more and more businesses.

Most electronic mail systems announce that mail is waiting when you log on or when you specifically check to see if you have mail waiting. Other electronic mail programs have a feature that causes the terminal or computer to beep and flash a message when electronic mail arrives. It's like having the letter carrier ring the doorbell as he drops the mail into the door slot.

When you use electronic mail, you can get replies and answers to questions much more quickly. When I worked for Digital Equipment Corporation, I would often communicate with engineers and instructors in Germany and England. The time difference between Colorado and London or Munich made telephone calls impractical and difficult, and the mails were much too slow. I'd leave an electronic mail message in the afternoon for someone in Germany, long after that person had gone home for the day. That person would come to work in the morning and answer my message while I was still asleep. When I'd come to work and log on to my system, I'd find the answer to the question I'd asked the day before.

And distance doesn't have to be involved. While working for the same electronics firm, I'd often find I couldn't get a timely appointment with the group engineering manager because of his busy schedule. I'd leave mail for him on the system and get replies the same day. Sometimes I'd log into the system from my home computer, leave mail for him, and get an immediate response. He'd be working at home, too, on his computer, and would answer my query right away.

Other electronic aids to business communication.

Electronic bulletin boards and information services such as GEnie, Compuserve, The Source, Dialog, Knowledge Index, and Dow Jones Information Retrieval are sources of information business people use every day. But these agencies also provide electronic mail services which allow you to communicate electronically with people all over the country. The people you send mail to don't have to be part of your company, on your company's mail net. They just have to be subscribers to one of these national services. This service allows you to send and receive mail without the delay and expense of overnight or express mail.

The last word in final copy.

These then are some of the tools you can use to prepare and send messages in the business world today. Although there seem to be many ways to get your message in to your reader, you still need a message that meets the criteria of Purpose, Audience, and Audience Needs. No amount of computer power or electronic gadgetry will remove that responsibility from your shoulders. You must develop a disciplined approach to writing messages to type, print, or mail electronically. It doesn't matter how a message arrives. If its is poorly written, it won't get the job done. If it is well written, it will.

Chapter 11

Your Writing Future

BECAUSE WRITING IS a skill activity like playing some sport or musical instrument, the more you practice, the better you get. Just as you get rusty during the off season or during times when you can't play a sport, you get rusty when you don't write. Higher performance in writing requires dedicated effort and practice. If you have had a break, say from high school or college, and then have started to write again, you have noticed how hard it is to get started.

In this chapter I'll try to leave you with some techniques you can practice to improve your business writing. The best advice I can give, though, is to write often and concentrate on making your writing work for you. Make sure you concentrate on Purpose, Audience, and Audience Needs. Then use the process I've used in this book, making sure you revise first for structure, then for readability, grammar, punctuation, and spelling. If you don't practice these basics, you'll find it tough to improve.

You must decide that you want to improve your writing style and your ability to communicate. Realizing that those who get ahead in business are invariably those who communicate well should be incentive enough. Pick an area you think needs improvement, and work on it. If you were playing golf and had trouble putting, you'd probably spend some time on the putting green. Do the same thing with your writing.

If you have trouble with your punctuation, spend some time with a book which addresses punctuation. Focus on that aspect of your writing as you revise the second draft. Make one pass through each document with punctuation as the sole error you are trying to root out. Don't worry about it until the second draft, though. Doing so would be like worrying about your putting technique as you are standing in the sand trap trying to get the ball up on the green.

Immediate and nearby help with your writing.

Don't discount finding help for your writing problems among your school or office mates. If you know someone whose reports, memos, and letters seem effortless to read, go to that person and ask for help, particularly in a business environment. Often a person who writes well knows the Purpose, Audience, and Audience Needs of documents that typically go out of your office and can help with that aspect of your writing. Ask her or him to read your final drafts and make constructive comments about ways you can improve. Ask to see how his writing process works. Find out what techniques work and don't work for her.

No one has all the answers, but answers that work for one writer may work for another. You must explore all the techniques you can, to find those which work best for you. Sometimes techniques you reject at one time in your writing career work later because you have matured in some other aspect of your writing. Keep searching.

Some books to help you get better.

Rather than provide a bibliography at the end of this book, I'd like to recommend a few books to help you improve your writing throughout your business career. I'll discuss the books in the order of the writing process I've used in this book.

I've recently read one which suggests an alternate approach to getting started. The book is

Howard, V. A., and Barton J. H. *Thinking on Paper.* New York: Quill/William Morrow, 1986.

Howard and Barton say that trying to build an outline by thinking about the topic and writing words and phrases on a piece of paper is not as efficient for getting started as is just writing about the topic.

They claim that your first step should be to write down your thoughts in a sort of rambling essay. Start somewhere and keep writing until you tire of writing or have written everything you have to say about the topic. This starting process borrows from two books by Peter Elbow:

> Elbow, Peter. *Writing Without Teachers*. London: Oxford University Press, 1973.
> ———. *Writing with Power*. New York: Oxford University Press, 1981.

Elbow calls his approach freewriting. First, sit down with a topic in mind and write nonstop for ten or fifteen minutes. Then pick the good ideas from that exercise and write again for another ten or fifteen minutes, again picking the best ideas from the ones in this writing session. Continue this process until you have the material you need to get started on your first organized draft.

Howard and Barton's process is similar. Write about your topic in a freewheeling essay, letting your mind associate freely. This freewriting exercise allows you to capture ideas that might not turn up during a brainstorming session. At least not for some people. I've had students who complained bitterly to me that they can't seem to get started using the brainstorming and outlining method I've suggested. They have abandoned that process and have started by writing pages full of ideas. I've cautioned them that although that process will work, they must be willing to severely edit and rewrite. And severe editing and rewriting sometimes means throwing out almost everything and starting over with some of the ideas from the first writing exercise.

Those students who have been willing to impose that discipline on themselves have often done well using this process, but it's not for everyone. Many have trouble looking at five pages of written work, pulling a few ideas from it, and discarding the rest of it as just so much fodder. Howard and Baker, however, make a very good argument for using a similar process.

To use their process, start by writing freely on the subject until you have exhausted the topic. Then, take that writing and organize it, using arrows, numbers, cutting and pasting, or any other technique to show how the next draft should be organized. Next, use that first reorganized draft as a starting point to write another draft. Type this draft again, even if you could do the reorganization using the cut and paste function of the computer. Because retyping the entire draft allows you to reprocess the information as you type, you can add new ideas and rephrase old ones during the process.

The final step in their process is to use the second draft as the basis of a third draft, again typing the entire draft, although they are not as adamant here about completely retyping it. Perhaps the authors are aware that people who use word processors hate to retype something they have already entered into the machine. Once again, their rationale for retyping this draft is to allow the brain to reprocess the information another time.

Writing From Scratch: For Business suggests a starting place, one that provides you with some basic skills to use as a base for growth. But, if you have trouble getting started using the more traditional method I've suggested, you may want to try the procedure discussed in *Thinking on Paper*. Don't be afraid to pick and choose from these methods. Perhaps you could use Elbow's freewriting exercise to make notes, Howard and Barton's process to come up with a more complete set of ideas, and then my outlining and non-stop writing method to produce the first draft. Nothing is sacred or magic when it comes to writing process. Do what works for you.

Revising for readability, punctuation, and grammar.

Here are three parts of the writing discipline you'll never finish learning about. Just as golfers, even the pros, practice their driving, chipping, and putting, writers, no matter how experienced and polished, continue to work on revising for readability, punctuation, and grammar. Probably because these are the areas that are the hardest to get good at. As you work on these aspects of your writing, you will establish your style, the voice that speaks to your readers. You can learn to hear your voice, but your ear needs to be kept in tune or it won't "hear" the subtle changes required to communicate at your best.

One book to use as a bible for style is an old standard. William Zinsser, himself a fine non-fiction writer, says that every serious writer should read this book at least once every year, and its beauty is that it's small. The book?

Strunk, William, Jr. and White, E. B. *The Elements of Style.* 3rd Edition. New York: MacMillan Publishing Co., 1979.

The first section of this book provides rules, simply stated, with examples of most of the punctuation and grammar problems you are likely to encounter. Each rule is stated clearly in the table of contents, but if you need more information, just turn to the page listed for a discussion and examples. Often just a glance at the table of contents will answer your question. The examples in the text show each error and its correction, so you can compare your own problem to the example.

The last section, "An Approach to Style," gives advice that any writer, no matter how experienced or skilled, can use. Here you'll find a set of rules, stated positively and briefly, with some explication of each. As you feel more comfortable with your writing skills, refer to these suggestions and incorporate them into your personal style.

Although William Zinsser, as I mentioned earlier, recommended that every writer read Strunk and White's "little book" once a year, he has written a book on writing that I read once a year. I follow the guidance he gives in this book, especially in the area of editing and revising. His book is

Zinsser, William. *On Writing Well*. 3rd Edition. New York: Harper & Row Publishers, 1988.

Part I of *On Writing Well* is called "Principles" and discusses elements of writing such as style, words, and usage. The words of advice here come from a practicing writer, words bearing the stamp of authority, words smelling of sweat, not the mustiness of a university library. He makes his living writing non-fiction, so he knows the difficulty of doing what he says you must do to become a good writer, but he also knows the pleasure of seeing words communicate clearly and concisely to the reader. His chapter called "Bits & Pieces" distills his years of writing, editing, and revising into notes of wisdom for every writer.

Why an informal writing style works.

Why, you might ask, is the writing style recommended in this book, one that is informal and even chatty, better than the more formal style Miss Grundy asked for—excuse me, demanded from you—in high school? Why are my suggestions any better than her rules? Are questions of style and readability really matters of personal preferences, or are there some empirical data to validate our writing choices? A friend of mine has examined these areas in researching his doctoral dissertation and published his research so we all have access to it. Easy to read and filled with supporting facts, his book is

Bailey, Edward P., Jr. *Writing Clearly: A Contemporary Approach.* Columbus, Ohio: Charles E. Merrill Publishing Company, 1984.

In the first part of *Writing Clearly,* Bailey deals with concepts like "crucial misconceptions," "how we write," and "how we read." Using the research discussed in this part of the book as a foundation, he provides writing guidelines that suggest adopting an informal writing style for your business writing. And you will see that Bailey's advice is echoed by Strunk and White and Zinsser in their books. Strunk learned these lessons as a teacher, White and Zinsser as writers. Perhaps they knew intuitively that a less formal style is correct, even if they didn't have laboratory proof, just their experience. Bailey gathered research others had done in laboratories and classrooms over many years and applied it to the writing and reading process to prove scientifically what Strunk, White, and Zinsser had known and written about the craft of writing. This book describes the writing you'll find on the editorial pages of the *Wall Street Journal, New York Times, Los Angeles Times, Time, Newsweek,* and other well-written and well-edited periodicals. If you want to feel more comfortable with an informal writing style and the decisions you make as you write, read this book. There's magic in the phrase "the research in the field says. . . ." When those who criticize your writing as being too informal learn that informal writing communicates better than pompous, bureaucratic, jargon-filled prose, they usually relent and start using that style themselves.

A book that shows the whole process

If you want to learn to write better, seeing a writer's struggle with the initial concept of a piece of writing, the brainstorming and outlining process, writing and revising the various drafts, and finally polishing the final copy is worth the price of admission. If I didn't believe that, I would not have asked you to watch my struggle with the four pieces of correspondence I've written for you in this book. Another book whose author asks you to watch this struggle is

Pratt, John Clark. *Writing From Scratch: The Essay.* Lanham, MD: Hamilton Press, 1987.

Pratt deals with the process of selecting ideas, narrowing those ideas to a manageable few, and then forming a workable structure for an essay with those remaining ideas. Much of the book focuses on his struggle with these ideas, and you get to see him make decisions and learn why he made them. He also lets you see his drafts with their initial warts and zits. Then he lets you see how he polishes each draft into a final essay that discusses a "not-really" affair he had one summer.

Learn to write better by reading more.

One final way to improve your writing is to read widely. Look around at the literature in your field to find writers whose articles and books read easily and communicate well? Read books by authors like John McPhee, Lewis Thomas, Loren Eiseley, and Jay Gould who make difficult scientific concepts easy to understand. Look at their style, their use of varied sentence structures, simple language, familiar concepts, analogy, and adopt some of their techniques in your own business writing. Read articles in well edited business school journals such as the *Harvard Business Review*. Many of the articles are written by executives who have been successful because they communicate well, in speech and on paper.

When you read for pleasure or for information, note what works and doesn't work in what you read. Analyze sentences that you have to read two or three times to understand. How could you rewrite them to make them communicate easily and quickly? When you read a paragraph that really communicates, go back through it to find the keys to its style and language. Why did you learn so quickly from it? How did the writer make the difficult seem simple? Imitate good writers with your own writing until you incorporate their best features into your own style.

A final word of encouragement

Practice, practice, practice. Writing takes more writing to become good writing. You must be conscious of your style and always be ready to revise and edit to make it better. Discover what works and doesn't work for you. Use what works. Wanting to write better is 90 percent of the fight. The other 10 percent is practice, practice, practice.

And that's about all I can tell you about business writing. The appendix of this book has the three memos and one letter to Star Fleet I wrote as I discussed my writing process in this book. Look them over. Feel free to criticize them, to find better ways of writing them, to find more graceful ways of saying things. I know they are not perfect; no piece of writing is. I think, however, they would do the job they were intended to do, and they meet the Killer Rules of Purpose, Audience, and Audience Needs.

Good luck, God speed, have fun in your career in the business world.

Appendix

Final Memos and Letters

HERE ARE THE memos to Bob Hollowell, Steve Berg, the purchasing department, and the letter to Admiral Mary Van Gordon. To return to my original metaphor, I started showing you a process for business writing, and these are the result of the maneuvers I've demonstrated while you watched, listened, and followed me through on the controls. No instructor can ever demonstate the perfect maneuver, and sometimes instructors watch their students fly even better than they do. If you perform these maneuvers better than I've done, I'll be happy and pleased.

To: **Bob Hollowell**   **15 September 2213**

From: <Your name>

Subject: **Plans for New Glues on the Model 1A Phaser Production Line**

Background

Star Fleet started having problems with our Model 1A Phaser when they installed new teleporters on new fleet cruisers. The old teleporters

161

decompose matter to the molecular level while the new teleporters decompose it to the atomic level. Apparently, reducing matter to the atomic level in areas with strong magnetic fields sometimes causes matter to be improperly reassembled and has caused the problems with the glue in the Model 1A Phaser.

We have been using the same glues in the Model 1A Phaser for the past three years with no problems. Star Fleet has phasers which have been teleported 1000 times with no reduction in the tensile or shear strength of the glues. With the new atomic level teleporters, however, the glues in the phasers have failed after fewer than 25 teleportations. This is obviously not satisfactory for either Star Fleet or Kiowa.

The materials lab has worked for three months to come up with new glue formulas to fix the problem. The new formulas have survived 10,000 teleportations and 10 times the normal testing to Star Fleet specs with no failures.

Production Changes

Fortunately, we'll have only a few changes to make to use the new glues:

- Three new gluing machines will replace older ones at the same stations on the line.

- The assembly procedures are very similar to the ones now in use.

- There is a slight difference in the curing process for the new glue.

The new curing process involves changes in temperature and time, not equipment or process. We'll conduct a short training class on October 15, 2213, to show the assemblers the new procedures. The lab people who developed the glue will train the production supervisors in the new processes. The supervisors will conduct the production classes.

I'll write a memo with appropriate attachments to Steve Berg, the production line manager, to provide details of training schedules, installation and production procedures, and machine operation.

Instructions for Purchasing

I'm writing a memo for purchasing to alert them to buy the three new gluing machines from Interglactic Industrial Equipment Corporation and to order the new glues from Acme Glue Products Company, Inc. I'll include monthly order rates for the glues in that memo.

Financial Effects of New Gluing Process

I've used the current plan in which we build 10 K phasers over the next three years for Star Fleet as a base to compute the unit cost increases:

- New gluing machines add $0.92

- Improved glue adds   0.01

- Labor costs   0.00

We've already delivered 3.7 K phasers to Star Fleet and will have to call them back to reglue them with the improved glue. One hundred and fifty phasers have failed in service. I expect another 150 to fail before we can replace them with new phasers. Here are the unit costs to repair the phasers already in service:

- 150 failed phasers $50.37

- 150 phasers likely to fail   50.37

- 3.4 K repaired at factory   20.25

We expect to repair the 3.4 K phasers at a rate of 1700 per month, which should get all phasers repaired and back in service in two months after we start the repair cycle. We'll need to work the details of this cycle with Star Fleet. For the time being, we can increase our production rate slightly and use the excess to replace failed units from the field.

The added cost of the new gluing process for the Model 1A Phaser product line is:

- Cost of new machines $9,200.00

- Added cost of glue   100.00

- Repair of existing units   15,111.00

Total Added Cost   **$24,411.00**

Total per unit Cost   **$2.44**

This will reduce the profit per unit from $53.74 to $51.30. I've not included the R & D costs in the figures because we can spread those across all our deep space product lines, making the delta cost minimal.

As you can see, installing the new machines and using the new glue will have a relatively small effect on our profit forecasts for the Model 1A Phaser product line. Because of this small effect, I've included a recommendation about how to handle the charges to Star Fleet.

Recommendation

My recommendation is that we tell Star Fleet about the new glue, give them the data on the testing we've done, and tell them we'll absorb the additional cost of manufacture and retrofit of phasers already in service.

The glue we have been using in the Model 1A Phasers meets all Star Fleet specs, and none have failed in service except with the new teleporters. We could charge our additional costs to Star Fleet and be within our legal rights. Our phasers, however, are failing in service and that hurts our reputation for quality. The delta cost to fix the problem doesn't cut into our profit margin very much, and the glue we've developed gives us a competitive advantage we can exploit immediately in other deep space products.

If you have any questions on the data or procedures I've outlined in this memo, please don't hesitate to call me at extension 5798.

To: **Steve Berg**   **17 September 2213**

From: <Your name>

Subject: **New Production Procedures for New Glues**

This memo describes production processes affected by the new gluing
process. Specifically, the memo covers:

- Schedules and resources

- Installation procedures for the new machines

- New gluing procedures for each station

- Curing procedures

- Machine loading procedures

All management information is contained in the first section of this memo.
Installation procedures, the new gluing procedures, curing procedures, and
machine loading procedures are to be included in the process books at each
station on the line.

Schedules and Resources

We need to change to the new gluing procedure as soon as possible, and the
schedules and resources required are tight. We must get the line personnel
trained as quickly as possible and get the new machines installed quickly.
Here are the dates and location for the key events:

- All production supervisors will be trained on the new processes on
  October 12, 2213. Bob Gates of R & D will conduct the training in the
  lab where the prototype machines are located.

- Training for those assemblers who will use the gluing process will be on
  Wednesday, October 15, 2213. Their supervisors will conduct the
  training. This training will also be in the lab where we have prototype
  machines available.

- The new machines will be installed on the line on Saturday, November 1,
  2213. These machines replace the three machines now on the line and
  those stations will require a minimum of reconfiguration. The major
  difference is the location of mounting holes and brackets.

- The cutover date for the new gluing process is Monday, November 3, 2213.

The new gluing procedure requires the same number of assemblers as the process you are now using, so there will be no change in head count.

Unit cost increase

The cost-per-unit increases slightly with the new process, due mainly to the cost of the new machines. Since that is a capital equipment cost, we'll amortize it over the next three years. Using an amortized cost equation, the increased costs per unit are:

- New gluing machines add $0.92

- Improved glue adds   0.01

- Labor adds   0.00

The cost per unit goes up to $2.44 when we include the cost of repairing phasers which have failed in service. Transportation costs account for that increase. The bottom line is that the profit per unit will slip from the currently planned $53.74 to $51.30. I've already notified Bob Hollowell of this figure and have made recommendations about recovering the increased costs.

Installation Procedures

The installation and checkout procedures for the new machines are simple and should require less than one day for all three machines. Two of the machines are large ones to replace those at stations 3 and 15. The other is a small one to replace the one at station 11. I've included step-by-step instructions for installation in a separate section of this memo. The instructions are ready for you to put in the process books at each station. The installation requires no special tools, only those our facilities maintenance people carry in their toolboxes.

New Gluing Procedures

The gluing procedures contained in this memo assume that assemblers who work at stations 3, 11, and 15 will be trained on October 15, 2213. We'll start using these procedures on November 3, 2213. Because the procedures are so similar to the current ones, the number of assemblers is exactly the same. The checklists attached at the end of this memo contain the procedures for each station. The curing process for all three stations is at the end of the gluing procedures and replaces the one now in the process books for each station.

New Curing Process

The curing process is a bit longer than the old process, but is the same for all three stations. We'll use the same ovens, but the curing temperature and time are different from the old ones. I've included the procedures for the new curing process at the end of this memo for you to include in the process books for stations, 4, 12, and 16.

Machine Loading Procedures

The new machines have a different loading process. The process, however, is simple and contained in a short checklist at the end of this memo. The checklist replaces the one now included in the process books for stations 3, 11, and 15.

Machine Maintenance Procedures

Routine cleaning and maintenance procedures for the three machines are included in the Installation and Operations Manual that comes with each machine. I have not included additional procedures, as the ones in the manual are sufficient. Use those procedures to schedule cleaning and maintenance on the machines.

Installation Procedure

Two of the machines are larger ones, replacing those at stations 3 and 15. The other is a small one to replace the machine at station 11. The connections to electrical power are standard, and the power lines now in place will be used on the new machines. The largest task necessary for the installation of all three machines is to locate new holes, drill them, install the mounting brackets, and attach the machines to the mounting brackets. You'll need no special tools. The installation process for all three machines is as follows:

Tools needed

¼ inch electric drill with ½ inch drill bit

Large screwdriver

Two ⅜ inch socket wrenches with 1 inch sockets

Small Phillips head screwdriver

Unpacking the gluing machine

You'll find five items in each of the shipping containers:

A large foam box containing the gluing machine

A smaller foam box containing the mounting bracket

One plastic bag with four ½ inch mounting bolts and nuts

One plastic bag with twelve ¼ inch bolts and nuts

An Installation and Operation Manual

If any parts are missing, call <Your name> at 5798.

Installing the mounting bracket

1. Locate the center of the current mounting bracket and use that as the center of the new mounting bracket. The new bracket is several inches larger than the old one. Make sure the open side of the new bracket faces the operator's position, directly in front of the machine.

2. Mark and drill four holes through the wood workbench area and the steel frame of the workbench.

3. Clean the drill shavings from the area and remove burrs from the wood and metal edges.

4. Mount the bracket with the four bolts that were provided, put the nuts on the bolts, and tighten them finger tight. You'll snug them down after the machine has been bolted to the bracket.

Mating the machine to mounting bracket

1. Lower the gluing machine into the mounting bracket so the red power switch faces the open end of the bracket. The open end of the bracket and the power switch should both face the operator station.

2. Place one ¼ inch mounting bolt through the end holes on each leg of the mounting bracket and through the corresponding holes in the gluing machine. You should have six bolts in place.

3. Put nuts on the end of each of these bolts and tighten them finger tight. This will help align the machine and ease the installation of the remaining bolts.

4. Place the remaining bolts through the mounting bracket, place nuts on them, and make them finger tight.

5. Tighten all 12 bolts you have just installed.

6. Now square the entire machine and mounting bracket with the workbench and tighten the four large mounting bolts. This completes the installation of the machine.

Connecting electric power to the machine

1. Make sure the circuit breaker is OFF to the power cables you will connect to the gluing machine.

2. Make sure the red power switch on the front of the machine is OFF.

3. Turn to page 3 of the Installation and Operation Manual that you found in the box to locate the power junction box, shown at the lower left of figure 2. Remove the cover.

4. Connect the three power leads to lugs T1, T2, and T3.

5. Connect the green ground lead to the ground lug marked GND, just below the three power lugs.

6. Replace the cover of the power junction box.

7. Place power on the machine by moving the power circuit breakers for the circuit back to ON. This completes the connection of electrical power to the machine.

Machine checkout procedure

1. Turn to page 6 of the Installation and Operation Manual that came with the machine and follow the procedure there titled "Initial Checkout and Setup."

2. Use the troubleshooting charts in chapter 5 if you encounter difficulties. If you have problems you can't fix, call <Your name> at 5798.

3. When through with the procedure, turn the machine back ON using the red power switch on the front of the machine. (The front of the machine faces the operator position.) Leave the machine ON over the weekend to let temperatures stabilize to factory operating conditions. This concludes the installation process.

Station 3: Gluing Process

This process assumes normal routing of parts to station 3 and normal procedures to insert parts into the robotic arms which present and hold the parts for gluing. It also assumes that assemblers will use the glue loading procedures in the process book.

Starting each shift

1. Turn the red power switch to ON.

2. Turn the heater switch to ON.

3. Check the heater temperature setting to 370 degrees.

4. Press the mixing switch and allow 10 minutes for proper glue mixing. After ten minutes, the glue machine is ready to operate.

Station 3: Gluing the PCB laminations

1. When the robot arms present the first lamination, press the #1 key on the operator panel.

2. When the robot arms present the second lamination, press the #1 key again.

3. When the robot arms clamp the laminations and load the IC chips, press the #2 key.

4. When the robot arm presents the power supply chip, press the #3 key.

5. When the robot arm presents the right edge connector assembly, press the #4 key.

6. When the robot arm presents the left edge connector assembly, press the #5 key.

This completes the gluing of the PCB assembly. The robot arm clamping the PCB will release the clamps and put the completed assembly into the curing holder. When the holder is full, take it to the curing oven at station 4.

Station 11: Gluing Process

This process assumes normal routing of parts to station 11 and normal procedures to insert parts into the robotic arms which present and hold the parts for gluing. It also assumes that assemblers will use the glue loading procedures in the process book.

Starting each shift

1. Turn the red power switch to ON.

2. Turn the heater switch to ON.

3. Check the heater temperature setting to 370 degrees.

4. Press the mixing switch and allow 10 minutes for proper glue mixing. After ten minutes, the glue machine is ready to operate.

Station 11: Gluing the Chassis Assembly

1. When the robot arms presents the PCB and chassis assembly, press the #1 key.

2. When the robot arm presents the trigger mount assembly, press the #2 key.

3. When the robot arms present the left and right multi-chip accelerator assemblies, press the #3 key.

4. When the robot arm presents the forward focusing ring, press the #4 key.

5. When the robot arm presents the rear focusing ring, press the #6 key.

This completes the gluing of the chassis assembly. The robot arm will put the completed assembly into the curing holder. When the holder is full, take it to the curing oven at station 12.

Station 15: Gluing Process

This process assumes normal routing of parts to station 15 and normal procedures to insert parts into the robotic arms which present and hold the parts for gluing. It also assumes that assemblers will use the glue loading procedures in the process book.

Starting each shift

1. Turn the red power switch to ON.

2. Turn the heater switch to ON.

3. Check the heater temperature setting to 370 degrees.

4. Press the mixing switch and allow 10 minutes for proper glue mixing. After ten minutes, the glue machine is ready to operate.

Station 15: Final assembly

1. When robot arm #1 presents the lower clam-shell assembly, press the #1 key.

2. When the robot arm #2 presents the trigger assembly, press the #2 key.

3. When robot arm #3 presents the lithium crystal power pack, press the #3 key.

4. When robot arm #2 presents the power adjustment switch, press the #4 key.

5. When robot arm #3 presents the upper clam-shell assembly, press the #5 key.

This completes the gluing of the final assembly. Robot arm #2 will place a clamp on the assembly and put the completed assembly into the curing holder. When the curing holder is filled, take it to the curing oven at station 16.

Curing Process for stations 4, 12, and 16

Use this process on all curing ovens:

At the beginning of each shift

1. Place the check thermometer into the oven and turn the oven power switch ON.

2. Set the oven temperature digital display to 1200 degrees.

3. Let the oven heat for ten minutes after the green READY light comes on.

4. Make sure the check thermometer reads 1200 degrees.

5. If the check thermometer does not read 1200 degrees, add or subtract the number of degrees to or from the 1200 to the oven temperature digital display.

6. Allow the oven to stabilize for 10 minutes after the green READY light comes on, and repeat steps 4 and 5.

   When the check thermometer reads 1200 degrees, the oven is ready for curing.

Procedures for curing parts

1. Open oven door and place one holder of glued parts into the center of the oven.

2. Close the door and press the HEAT ACCEL button.

3. Set the curing timer to 3 minutes.

4. Note that the timer starts to count down from 3 minutes when the red CURING light comes on.

5. When the red CURING light goes out, the door lock will automatically unlock. Remove the curing holder from the oven and place on the cooling bench.

   NOTE: This completes the curing process. Ensure that the curing holders are not moved for at least 30 minutes after they have been placed on the cooling bench.

Machine Loading Procedures

Each machine has a counter which displays the number of glue applications
made since the last time the glue reservoir was filled. Although the reservoir
at each machine contains approximately 110 glue applications, you should
fill the machine when the counter on the monitor shows 100 glue
applications have been made. The monitor normally displays a steady
reading, but will flash the number 100 when that number has been reached.
Use the following procedure to load the machine.

1. Turn the ARM switch to standby.

2. Open the Blue cover on the large reservoir.

3. Fill the reservoir to the FILL LINE with base contained in the Blue
   bottle.

4. Close and lock the Blue cover on the large reservoir.

5. Open the Red cover on the small reservoir.

6. Fill the reservoir to the FILL LINE with glue contained in the Red
   bottle.

7. Close and lock the Red cover on the small reservoir.

8. Turn the ARM switch to ARM.

This completes the procedure for loading glue in the gluing machines. If, at
the beginning of a shift or at some other convenient time, the counter shows
fewer than 100 applications, you may load the machine using these
procedures. Don't go below 100 applications on the counter because glue
quality may be compromised.

To: **Purchasing Department**   **17 September 2213**

From   <Your name>

Subject: **Equipment and Supplies Purchase Requirements**

This memo contains order information for gluing machines, glue, and other supplies for the Model 1A Phaser Product Line. It includes the no-later-than dates for receiving the machines and initial shipments of glues.

Capital Equipment Requirements

You will need to order three gluing machines from Interglactic Industrial Equipment Corp. (IIEC) We have been working with them on our requirements, and they have supplied us with prototype machines for process testing. We need to have one each of the following glue machines on hand no later than Thursday, October 30, 2213:

   IIEC Model GM-1701-L-03

   IIEC Model GM-1701-L-15

   IIEC Model GM-1701-S-11

These models have been specifically programmed for operations at stations 3, 11, and 15 on the Model 1A Phaser Product Line.

Production Supplies Requirements

Please order these glue supplies from Acme Glue Products Company, Inc., for the new gluing process on the Model 1A Phaser Product Line. We'll need the initial order no later than Thursday, October 23, 2213. The first delivery at the monthly reorder rates should be no later than November 30, 2213, and each monthly delivery no later than the last day of the month.

Acme Part Number	Initial Quantity	Monthly Reorder Rate
Acme GL-1701-03	14 Liters	12 Liters
Acme GL-1701-11	05 Liters	04 Liters
Acme GL-1701-15	22 Liters	18 Liters
Acme BM-1701-29	37 Liters	30 Liters
Acme Solvent #33	20 Liters	15 Liters

Please have all machines and initial supplies delivered to the Phaser Product Line in-plant warehouse and notify Henry Lancing at extension 5798 when they arrive. Handle monthly supply orders in the normal way.

Contact for more information

Before November 1, 2213, contact <Your name> at 5798

After November 1, 2213, contact Steve Berg at 5799

Kiowa Arms Manufacturing Company, Inc.
Douglas Rock, Colorado 80999

18 September 2213

Dear Admiral Van Gordon:

As you know, Model 1A Phasers have suddenly been failing in service. We had our Testing Lab look into the problem and come up with a solution. Here's a discussion of the problem, our solution to the problem, and the plan for implementing the solution.

Why our Phasers failed in service.

The Testing Lab noted immediately that the phasers in question had been through fewer than 25 teleportations and came from Star Fleet cruisers which use the new teleporters. These teleporters decompose matter to the atomic level rather than to the molecular level as the older teleporters did. The lab engineers suspected that the molecular structure of the glue in the phasers was somehow being changed, something no one expected. Tests showed that there was a subtle but important change occurring in the glue after about 15 teleportations. Phasers that failed averaged about 20 teleportations, but one had failed with only 17.

How we fixed the problem with the glue.

Working with the Acme Glue Products Company, Inc., our R & D Lab came up with a glue that has a slightly stronger molecular bonding than the glue we now use. We tested the glue in an atomic level teleporter, similar to your new teleporters, and found no change in the glue's molecular structure after 10,000 teleportations. We then took the phasers which had been through 10,000 teleportations and tested them at ten times Star Fleet qualification specifications. Not one phaser failed. We're sure we have this problem fixed.

How we'll fix phasers now in service.

We'll ship the first 150 phasers to come off the production line with the new glue directly to Star Fleet cruisers to replace ones which have failed. Given the time necessary to get the new phasers to the fleet, we expect another 150 failures before we can replace all phasers now in service. We'll replace phasers which fail immediately from production stock. We'll replace them in space and provide several spares to count against final replacement numbers.

How we'll retrofit the rest of the fleet.

Our plan is to replace the phasers on each cruiser as it comes into space dock for periodic maintenance and refitting. We'll then replace the glue in those phasers and return them to service. We can do this and still maintain the delivery schedule we agreed to in our contract. That schedule has us delivering 10,000 phasers over the next three years. The replacement program will be small compared to the total program, so we will absorb that cost.

Why are we absorbing the cost?

The obvious reason for our absorbing the cost is to show that we are concerned about the quality of our products, even if a failure in a product is not a direct result of our materials, workmanship, or design. Another reason for this gesture of good will is that we will use this new glue in other products we manufacture for deep space, products like medical kits, atmospheric sampling stations, and other weapons which will undergo teleportation.

I hope this letter puts your mind at rest about the Model 1A Phaser problem and answers questions you may have had. If you do have any other questions, please feel free to call me about them.

Sincerely,

Bill Cutler, Vice President
Customer Service
Kiowa Arms Manufacturing Corp., Inc.